Bobbie's Organic Planet

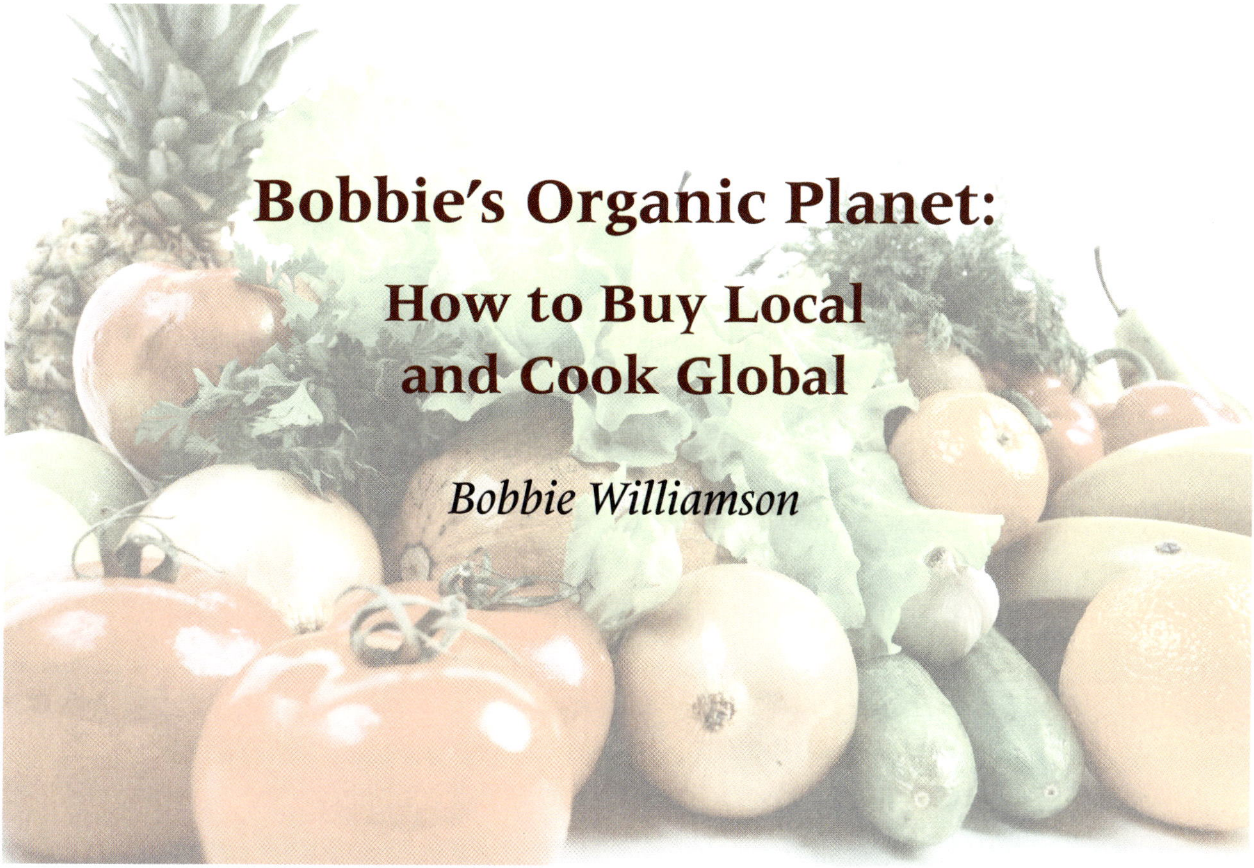

Bobbie's Organic Planet:

How to Buy Local and Cook Global

Bobbie Williamson

A.R.E. Press • Virginia Beach • Virginia

Copyright © 2009
by Bobbie Williamson

1st Printing, July 2009

Printed in the U.S.A.

All rights reserved. No part of this book may be reproduced or transmitted in any form or by any means, electronic or mechanical, including photocopying, recording, or by any information storage and retrieval system, without permission in writing from the publisher.

A.R.E. Press
215 67th Street
Virginia Beach, VA 23451-2061

ISBN-13: 978-0-87604-575-6

Edgar Cayce Readings © 1971, 1993-2007
by the Edgar Cayce Foundation.
All rights reserved.

Cover design by Christine Fulcher

To my two most precious and inspiring daughters, Brooke Bovay Bandler and Bree Bovay, who have always stood by me through the good and the bad. I love them dearly and cannot imagine a day without them! I cannot forget my mum, Bebe Gregory Williamson, and my grandmum, Elsa Payson Caldwell, who taught me so much.

Contents

Acknowledgments ix

The Chef: Bobbie Williamson xi

Edgar Cayce's Philosophy on Food xiii

Stocking Your Pantry xv

Herbs and Edible Flowers xix

Delightful Dips and Hors d'Oeuvres 1

Salads in the Raw and Not So Raw 23

Vinaigrettes and Dressings 55

Warm Your Soul Soups 75

Vegetarian Fare 95

From the Seas and Rivers 117

Of Fowl and Lamb 135

Ever So Slightly Sweets 159

Menu Suggestions 177

Our Planet and Food 179

Index 183

Acknowledgments

I now understand why authors have so many people to thank after having completed a book. This project is the culmination of many friends, family, and colleagues leading me to do something I never thought I could do, but always dreamed of!

First of all, I would like to thank the entire staff (past and present) of the A.R.E. and the Edgar Cayce Foundation; in particular, Maryann Belgrand, Richard Boyle, Leslie Cayce, the late Joe Dunn, Joan Grasser, Shay Harrison, Kathryn Kelly, Cassie McQuagge, Cathy Merchand, Jennie Taylor-Martin, Marianna Theo, and Kevin Todeschi. They have been inspirational in ways they may never know.

Then, there is Doris Van Auken, my editor. I had no idea how important an editor was until we started working together on this project. Doris has shown me infinite patience while trying to decipher my right-brained way of thinking. I can honestly say that God gave me a gift when Doris was asked to work with me. I will be forever grateful and wish to thank her from the bottom of my heart.

And then, there are the dear ones in many countries who have been with me for years, especially my sisters, Jennifer Williamson Mackay and Maris Williamson Pascal, and friends Susie and John Burke, Carmen and Francesco Gay-Crossier, Tina Williams, Nancy and Dennis Chrisbaum, Beedee MacMillan, Pauline Darling, Charlene Rodgers, Silvio Parodi, Romina Capdequi, Marita and Maamoun Tamer, Sherry Harden, and Molly Badger. I would also like to acknowledge my brother-in-law Chas Mackay and friend Cindy Cutler for supplying such wonderful photographs. I love you all. I would also like to thank the farmers of this earth for all they do to supply us with fresh food to nourish our body, mind, and spirit!

Jane Morrison is my best friend. Who else would trudge through fields of beets with me and then eat the beets cooked a thousand different ways? She has kept me calm and organized, using logic to document recipes while I cook what seems simple to me, after years of practice. Jane has followed me to local farmers markets in Virginia, Colorado, Connecticut, and North Carolina while I spend hours doing what I love to do—look at, touch, and buy the freshest produce available on a given day. Her next journey with me will be to all the beautiful markets in Switzerland and France. I hope there will be many more such journeys!

The Chef: Bobbie Williamson

I grew up in a family that put great emphasis on eating what I term *living* food. I do not remember eating much fast food and, to this day, will not touch it. I would much rather whip up something simple, even if I am eating on my own. Mealtimes bring back fond memories for me. We often had family and friends over to make it even more entertaining. Conversations were lively and animated, and that is most likely why I love to throw dinner parties!

I was brought up in the United States and Canada. Both of my maternal grandparents were great cooks, and they passed on that tradition to my beloved mother, Bebe Gregory Williamson. My family was also world-traveled, so our plates were often filled with uncommon dishes for my traditional baby boomer generation. Curries, South American spices, and Mediterranean foods were often served to me as a child, so my taste buds were well-developed at a very young age.

At the age of twenty-one and newly married, I moved to Geneva, Switzerland, where I was quickly introduced to the smallest refrigerators in the world and freezers the size of handkerchiefs. There were no fast-food restaurants, and everyone knew how to cook, including making one's own salad dressings. I had to shop daily to make our dinners. There were local markets in almost every village, and the grocery stores sold locally grown produce. However, stores and bakeries seemed to have the strangest hours: they were closed at noon and reopened again at 2 o'clock; they then closed again at 6:30. And they were closed on Sundays, as well. Only bakeries were open on Sunday. There were no 24-hour convenience shops to save the day.

Living in Switzerland meant that there were many trips to nearby countries, including France, Italy, Germany, Spain, and England. How I loved to experiment with new cuisines, and I started paying close attention to how regional dishes should really taste. That meant that I had to become adept at using herbs and spices. I started my lifelong habit of buying them wherever I traveled, to incorporate them into my food. My daughters now purchase spices for me on their world travels.

Moving to Jeddah, Saudi Arabia, expanded my horizons, as far as cooking is concerned. Going to the date souk (market) was like going back in time. There were huge mounds of differently aged dates, starting with the raw variety. Then, there was the vegetable souk, the fruit souk, the spice souk, and on and on. As I could not work (foreign women were not allowed to work unless nurses or flight attendants) and had to have a driver to get around (no women are allowed to drive), my girlfriends and I would make our outings to various souks.

A lot of my friends had live-in chefs from various countries. Food was the center of our universe, and one did not go to restaurants often in Saudi. There were no theaters, cinemas, or symphonies to attend. We relied on each other for entertainment, so once again, I found myself cooking for friends and loving it. It was actually one of the highlights of my life.

As with all expatriates living in the hottest country in the world, everyone traveled just to get away from the incredible heat. Trips to Turkey, Greece, Europe, the States, Southeast Asia, and other Middle Eastern countries were the norm. I did not complain.

Moving forward, while living in Geneva, I became interested in reading books written about various topics related to Edgar Cayce. As it was difficult to find a wide variety of these books in Geneva, I ordered a catalog from the Association for Research and Enlightenment (A.R.E.) in Virginia Beach, where I had spent the first nine years of my life. My daughter Brooke had returned from a vacation in New York about the same time the catalog arrived. She handed me a book by George Anderson called *We Don't Die*. I had received a conference schedule with my A.R.E. catalog, and when I opened it, there was a conference featuring George Anderson. So, in *my* mind, this was a *sign*. I decided to fly to Virginia Beach and attend a conference there. The George Anderson one was booked, so I went to the following one: "Finding Your Mission In Life."

Two days after arriving in Virginia Beach and feeling totally at home here, I phoned the girls in Geneva and announced that we were moving. As they say in Hollywood, the rest is history. My girls were fifteen and sixteen, and Switzerland was their home. Do not ask me about our departure at the Geneva Airport. About twenty incredulous friends were there to say good-bye. They just couldn't believe it! Four transatlantic crossings and five months later, the girls and I had moved to America! My girls cried the whole way over, and people must have thought I had kidnapped them.

I started volunteering at the A.R.E. once I got my girls settled into the American way of life. I loved the Cayce readings regarding food and soon realized that they made perfect sense and were actually quite similar to the very healthy Mediterranean diet I was used to. Eating locally grown and seasonal food was something I had done my whole life without knowing why it was so important. The readings explained much to me and highlighted proper food combining, which can be crucial to one's health.

I do believe that many of us come full circle in life. I was blessed throughout life to be a part of a family of wonderful souls, from all walks of life, who hold very similar values without necessarily being of the same religion or background. Also, my whole life, I wanted to write a book. Now I have had this wonderful opportunity to write one on what has become my passion—food!

I have had the opportunity to cook for many people who visit the A.R.E. from all over the world, as well as the many staff members who enjoy my food. Most recently, I have started teaching people how to cook tasty meals from scratch, and this is what I truly love doing. There is nothing quite like seeing the look on someone's face when he or she realizes how simply salad dressings can be made and the superior taste they add to any salad. Or when someone realizes how delicious homemade soups are over canned ones, yet require such little fuss. I hope to be traveling in the near future to teach more people how to take care of their health by cooking living and vibrant foods.

It is my desire that in reading this book, you will feel enticed to throw out your canned goods and start cooking. I hope you will experiment and introduce your loved ones to a whole new way of eating—one that is healthy and based on buying the very best produce you can find—and then fill your cooking with love to make your own creations! If my pots could talk, this is part of the story they would tell. Thank you and good luck!

Bon appetit!

Edgar Cayce's Philosophy on Food

> . . . for what we think and what we eat—combined together—*make* what we *are* physically and mentally.   288-38

Mr. Cayce was ahead of his time about many things. And, finally, people seem ready to listen to his wisdom in relation to diet. It's gratifying that many of his concepts are accepted by mainstream nutritionists and medical doctors today.

Cayce had no idea how forward-thinking he was when he spoke of the importance of eating locally grown and seasonal foods. Turn on just about any news channel or radio show these days, and these concepts will likely be topics of discussion. People are starting to become conscious that the out-of-season foods they buy have been shipped thousands of miles to get to our grocery stores. Added to the strain on the environment is the fact that eating foods transported long distances means that they are not fresh and that their nutritional value has been compromised, not to mention taste. But there is another health benefit to eating local foods that science and the health conscious may not be aware of, which is mentioned in the last sentence of the following reading:

> **Do not have large quantities of any fruits, vegetables, meats, that are not grown in or come to the area where the body is at the time it partakes of such foods. This will be found to be a good rule to be followed by all. This prepares the system to acclimate itself to any given territory.**   3542-1

At the time of the Cayce readings, farms were not peppered with harmful pesticides as they are now. Organically grown food was the norm, unlike today, so Cayce did not specify that food be consumed organically. However, if he were alive today, I feel certain that he would speak of the importance of eating pesticide-free foods. Sadly, too many farmers have been encouraged to use chemicals in order to have larger crop yields. This practice started during World War II, when there were food shortages.

So many children are starting puberty at a very young age now. It has been said that this is due in large part to the amount of hormones they ingest through dairy and meat products. If you can purchase locally raised/produced, hormone- and additive-free meat and dairy products, then all the better for your health, your family's health, and the health of our environment.

Cayce was an advocate of eating whole, preservative-free foods, with an emphasis on whole grains rather than processed ones; more fish, fowl, and lamb than red meat; more leafy green vegetables than starchy ones; and a daily diet composed of 80 percent alkaline-producing foods to 20 percent acid-producing foods. In general, most vegetables and fruits are alkaline-producing, and most grains, starches, meats, sweets, and no-nos are acid-producing.

Cayce said it this way:

> **But have rather a percentage of eighty percent *alkaline*-producing to twenty percent acid-producing foods. Then, it is well that the body not become as one that couldn't do this, that or the other; or as a slave to an idea of a set diet. Do not take citrus fruit juices *and* cereals at the same meal. Do not take milk or cream in coffee or in tea. Do not eat fried foods of any kind. Do not combine white bread, potatoes, spaghetti—or any two foods of such natures in the same meal.** 1568-2

There is great advice in this reading, especially for anyone who wishes to maintain health and a healthy weight and to ensure that one's family does, as well. Too many families eat pasta and white bread at the same meal, to be followed by a cane sugar dessert. And too many families eat fried and fast food regularly. Children in North America are battling obesity and childhood diabetes as never before. And the adult population fights its own battles with obesity and type 2 diabetes. By setting the example of eating a healthy, balanced diet, we help our children develop eating habits that will benefit them throughout their lives. As with so many issues in life, balance is the key.

> **The diet also should be considered—in that there is not an excess of acids or sweets, or even an excess of alkalinity . . .**
> **Hence there should be kept a normal, well-balanced diet that has proven to be right for the individual body . . .** 902-1

Fried foods are full of saturated fats, which by now, most people know are not beneficial for anyone. A diet heavy in saturated fats is associated with high cholesterol in the bloodstream. Further, if one's body is too acidic, it is prone to inflammatory, degenerative diseases, and viruses will thrive. And we know that our thoughts, emotions, and state of health have an effect on the digestive process. At long last, this is now acknowledged by modern science these many years later!

When we combine our foods properly, we put less stress on our digestive process, ensuring that our food can be more easily assimilated and digested and nutrients absorbed. It makes sense not to eat when one is upset, angry, or overtired. The body cannot digest what it is ingesting.

Perhaps in modern times the popular Mediterranean diet comes closest in approach to the Cayce diet. It is regarded as one of the healthiest in the world. And, certainly, if most of us followed it, we would be far more healthy. The Mediterranean diet encourages the consumption of unsaturated oils, such as olive and walnut; fruits, legumes, and vegetables; Omega-3 rich fish, as well as lamb and poultry; and whole grains.

Cayce takes this diet a step further by not only recommending that foods not be fried and that certain food combinations be avoided, but that heated oils not be used in cooking. When cooked, foods are to be baked, broiled, poached, or steamed—and vegetables cooked individually in their own juices.

Health is an individual choice, and we must choose what works best for ourselves. But, again, Cayce advised not getting too fixed on restrictions. I have tried to include wholesome recipes and suggestions compatible with healthy choices—which is the message of this book.

Stocking Your Pantry

Oh, how much healthier life can be when our refrigerator and pantry are well-stocked with fresh organic produce, dairy products, and garden herbs! The first piece of advice I give to anyone wanting to change one's lifestyle and start anew is to throw out any products containing high fructose corn syrup. Sadly, most Americans consume far too many refined sugars, which not only pack on the pounds but serve no nutritional value whatsoever. Certainly, children do not need to eat sugar-coated cereal. If you are serious about your health and that of your family's, get rid of these packaged cereals and snack foods filled with so many unhealthy ingredients one needs to be a scientist to decipher them.

Also, if you have been used to drinking carbonated drinks, take note that they are toxic and will eventually make you ill. Asked in a Cayce reading about the effects of consuming soft drinks, this was the unequivocal response: "*Do not* take any form of drinks that carry carbonated waters. The gases of these . . . are detrimental . . . " (1013-3) Interestingly, the coke syrup itself was said to have medicinal qualities. Drink filtered water and make your own iced teas and lemonades.

Shop on the outside aisles of supermarkets, and you will be more likely to stay healthy. The inside aisles are stacked with processed foods no one needs.

Dried herbs and spices should be kept in airtight containers in a cool, dark space away from sunlight. I like to keep my flour in the refrigerator, as I live in a humid climate and do not want any unwanted "visitors." Maple syrup should always be refrigerated upon opening, or mildew will form on top. The same goes for tomato ketchup and mayonnaise. Oils should never be refrigerated but kept in a space away from direct sunlight. They do become rancid, their shelf life only about six months even under favorable conditions.

Always buy the best quality ingredients—this does not necessarily mean that they will be the most expensive. Many supermarkets now market their own brands, and often these are made by top companies but sold at a more reasonable price.

Certain foods should definitely be consumed only if organic, as the conventional varieties are filled with pesticides. These items are italicized in *green* throughout the book to remind you of the importance of buying only organic. Yes, it would be great to be able to afford everything organically grown, but most families cannot do this. So, if anything, please ensure that you spend the extra money on these items and save on the doctor bills. Other less contaminated products that can be consumed non-organically are listed under "Conventional Products."

Not everyone has an old-fashioned pantry at home, but almost everyone has cupboard space. I have listed the ingredients I feel are useful to buy for the recipes throughout this book and in everyday cooking. By having necessary ingredients on hand, you can always throw something wonderful together at a moment's notice by being creative or by just following any of the simple recipes found in this book.

Essential Organic Products
Apples
Bell Peppers
Butter
Celery
Cherries
Coffee
Dairy Products—Milk, Cheese, Cream, Yogurt
Eggs
Grapes
Lettuce
Meat, Poultry, and Lamb
Nectarines
Peaches
Pears
Potatoes
Raspberries
Spinach and other greens
Strawberries
Tomatoes

As always, buy locally grown and in-season products as often as possible. You are doing much to help your local economy, not to mention helping your body—by the time one consumes vegetables and fruits shipped in from around the globe, such produce is not actually fresh and the nutritional value has declined tremendously. Also, once you start eating local, seasonal food, you will taste the difference and your taste buds will beg you to always humor them with great food!

Remember also that you are cutting down on your carbon footprint by making the choice to eat this way! To think of how much energy is consumed in shipping products from one part of the planet to another is mind-boggling. There are many statistics written about this and they are very depressing, but sometimes the truth hurts. Do your bit.

Conventional (non-organic) Products
Asparagus
Avocados
Bananas
Broccoli
Cauliflower
Corn
Kiwi Fruit
Mangos
Papaya
Pineapples
Peas (Sweet)

The Dry Pantry
Anchovy Paste
Cereals
   All Bran
   Whole Grain Cereals
   Shredded Wheat
Coconut Milk
Cold-Pressed Oils
   Olive
   Safflower
   Sesame
   Sunflower
   Walnut
Dried Beans and Lentils
Dried Fruits (unsulphured)
   Apricots
   Cherries
   Cranberries
   Dates
   Raisins
Dried Vegetables
   Mushrooms
   Sun-Dried Tomatoes
Flour
   Gluten-Free Flour
   Whole Wheat Flour
   Unbleached White Flour
Grains
   Bulgur
   Rice
   Arborio Rice
   Brown Rice
   Wild Rice

Jello
Knox Gelatin
Mustards
  Dijon
  Whole Grain
Olives
  Green
  Cured
Polenta
Pure Vanilla Extract
Rye Crisp
Sweeteners
  Local Honey
  Organic Beet Sugar
  Stevia
Tomatoes
  Canned Diced Tomatoes
  Canned Tomato Paste
Vinegars
  Apple Cider
  Balsamic
  Red Wine
Whole Wheat Pasta

HERBS AND SPICES

Dried Herbes
Basil leaves, Bay leaves, Coriander, Cumin, Dill Weed, Herbs de Provence, Marjoram, Oregano, Paprika, Parsley flakes, Rosemary, Saffron, Thyme, Za'atar

Pepper
  Black Peppercorns,
  Cayenne Pepper,
  White Pepper

Sea Salt

Spices
Allspice, Ground Cinnamon, Cinnamon Sticks, Ground Cloves, Ground Ginger, Ground Nutmeg, Turmeric

Fresh Staples
Applesauce
Butter (unsalted)
Cheese
  Feta
  Goat
Eggs
Fresh Herbs
Fruits
  Lemons
  Lemon Juice
Olives
  Cured
  Green
Maple Syrup
Mayonnaise
Milk
Nuts
  Almonds
  Walnuts
Pine Nuts
Rice Milk
Tomato Ketchup
Vegetables
  Carrots
  Celery
  Garlic
  Lettuce
  Onions
  Potatoes
  Sweet Potatoes
Seeds
  Sesame, Pumpkin, Sunflower
Soy Milk
Soy Yogurt
Yogurt

Suggested Cooking Gadgets and Equipment

Knives—A paring knife, a chef's knife, and a serrated knife for cutting bread are essential items to have on hand. The chef's knife should fit nicely in your hand.

Immersion Blender—a hand-held blender that is great for making salad dressings and sauces, and pureeing soups right in the pot.

Food Processor—saves an incredible amount of time in making dips and many recipes noted in this book.

Microplane—a great gadget for grating cheese and zesting lemons, limes, and oranges.

Toaster Oven—excellent for making croutons and for toasting nuts. Also a great way to save on your carbon footprint by not using an oven.

Salad Spinner—If you wash and dry your greens, this is a most useful item to have at home. Leaves will be dry and the salad dressing will adhere easier.

Mortar and Pestle—great for mincing garlic and making pastes/rubs. If you have the larger one, you can make your salad dressings in this handy device.

Pots and Pans

In the Cayce readings, the use of patapar paper (unbleached parchment paper) in cooking is highly recommended as well as cooking in granite (enameled ironware) and stainless steel. You will find that the best cookware on the market today is stainless steel. A cast-iron skillet, rice and vegetable steamer, pressure cooker, and wok are great items to have in the pantry, as well.

Herbs and Edible Flowers

HERBS

Fresh herbs enhance the flavors of any dish and are also used as garnishes. They are what make basic foods come alive. Fresh herbs are more delicate than dried herbs but add more flavor. The general rule of thumb is to substitute fresh herbs for dried ones in a ratio of 3 to 1. That is, use three times as much fresh herbs as you would dried herbs.

Fresh herbs should not be cooked for long and should be added at the end of the cooking process, as they can become bitter. Make sure your herbs are organic and planted in organic soil. Herbs have no protective skins, so any pesticides will be impossible to rinse off. Also, the organic variety will give you far more nutrients. Herbs are not just for flavor but have been used for medicinal purposes, fragrances, and sorcery for centuries. Most culinary herbs are indigenous to the Mediterranean region and thus require direct sunlight.

Experiment with fresh herbs and find what combinations best suit your palette. Borage grown near tomatoes gives the latter more taste and is great added to salads and soups. Adding fresh mint to butter beans or May peas is a great substitute for salt and pepper. Mint is also commonly paired with roast lamb in the Middle East and in England. Basil complements a fresh tomato salad, as does flat-leaf parsley. Lavender can make a normal butter cookie an exotic one for a tea party. Dill makes for a tasty garnish on freshly grilled salmon. Chives added to sour cream give a natural bite. Cilantro is commonly found in Asian, Italian, and Mexican cuisine.

Rosemary and fresh mint grow easily in the South, where I live, so I tend to use these two herbs often in my kitchen, as they proliferate wildly in my garden. Freshly cut rosemary placed in a small vase adds a delicious fragrance to my kitchen. I often add mint leaves to herbal teas in the summertime to make a great iced tea.

Herbes de Provence (provincial herbs) is an aromatic blend of herbs from the south of France. Rosemary, basil, oregano, marjoram, thyme, fennel, and sage are the traditional blend. My favorite one incorporates fresh lavender. Herbes de Provence is typically used in dishes from the Mediterranean and complements salads, chicken, lamb, and fish. This blend makes for a great rub combined with olive oil. My kitchen is never without a great quantity, and it sets any dish apart. My children religiously send me fresh supplies, or I buy my stash when visiting them in Europe.

Herbes de Provence is easily available in most grocery stores now. However, it is a rather pricey commodity outside of Europe. Here is a recipe that is easily made at home. The traditional manner of storing it is in terracotta jars, but glass ones will do fine, as well. This makes for a great gift to any host or hostess entertaining you.

Herbes de Provence
Makes 1/3 cup

1 tablespoon dried rosemary
1 tablespoon dried thyme
1 tablespoon dried sage
1 teaspoon dried lavender
1 teaspoon dried tarragon
1 teaspoon dried marjoram
1/2 teaspoon dried oregano
1/2 teaspoon dried mint
2 teaspoons dried crushed bay leaves

Mix together all of the ingredients and store in a terra cotta container or glass jar.

Za'atar is an Arabic term referring to any various local herbs of the mint family, including marjoram, oregano, and thyme. Green za'atar mixture is traditionally composed of dried thyme, toasted white sesame seeds, and sea salt. Red za'atar is made with dried thyme with sumac. Sumac is commonly found in Middle Eastern stores, or it can be ordered online.

    The following recipe is simple and tasty.

Za'atar

3 tablespoons toasted sesame seeds
2 tablespoons dried thyme
1 tablespoons dried marjoram
1/2-1 tablespoon powdered sumac

Mix ingredients together in a small bowl. Store in a glass jar away from light.

Here is a list of commonly grown fresh herbs to be added to your cuisine:

Basil
Bay Leaves
Borage
Chives
Cilantro
Dill
Fennel
Flat-leaf parsley
Lavender
Marjoram
Mint
Oregano
Rosemary
Sage
Tarragon
Thai basil
Thyme

EDIBLE ORGANIC FLOWERS
Edible flowers are perhaps my favorite living food decoration of all. Flowers are beautiful to look at in a vase, but try putting them atop a salad or interspersed on your hors d'oeuvres tray, and such a joyful and tasty touch is added. Just as said, they are truly edible. Do you remember as a kid finding a honeysuckle bush and sucking the nectar from its flowers?

It is easy to plant your own edible flowers in rows in your garden or just in clay pots. To be edible flowers, they must be grown in organic soil. You must never collect them by the side of the road or buy them at floral shops, for neither of these sources will provide safe flowers to eat. Wash the petals well and cut off the stems. Many organic markets sell these little delights, and some grocery stores stock them too, but give growing your own a try.

Not everyone likes the taste of flowers, so use them sparingly at first and find out which ones are suitable to your family. My personal favorites are nasturtium, pansies, and honeysuckle. Nasturtiums have a slight peppery taste and come in many hues. They also grow easily. Pansies are varied in color, as well, and honeysuckle is delicate and sweet, just like honey.

Listed below is a variety of common edible flowers you can choose from; however, there are many more. Look on the Internet to find a complete list.

Apple blossoms	Johnny-Jump-Ups
Apricot petals	Lavender
Bean Blossoms	Marigolds
Begonia	Nasturtiums
Calendula	Pansies
Carnations	Peach blossoms
Clover	Pear blossoms
Dandelions	Peonies
Daylilies	Primrose
Geraniums	Squash Blossoms
Honeysuckle	

Delightful Dips and Hors d'Oeuvres

I don't know anyone who does not like a great dip. Included in this section are unusual and easy-to-make ones. Dips do not have to be fattening to be good, and it is often a great way to introduce children and fussy ones to a variety of veggies.

Sadly, many American children and adults will only eat raw vegetables with store-bought Ranch dressing. This is not only filled with preservatives and sugar but has absolutely no nutritional value.

Try these recipes and start incorporating an array of crudités (raw vegetables) into your diet. Carrots, celery, broccoli, asparagus, yellow squash, zucchini, cauliflower, cucumbers, green beans, spring onions, radishes, cherry tomatoes, snow peas, and sweet peppers are full of flavor. Lightly steamed Brussels sprouts are also an option. And the more color you introduce into your diet, the healthier you will be. Once you start "playing" with the rainbow hues, you will feel like an artist and your plate will become your canvas.

In reading 2602-1, Cayce says:

Have at least one meal each day that includes a quantity of raw vegetables, such as cabbage, lettuce, celery, carrots, onions and the like. Tomatoes may be used in their season. Do have plenty of vegetables above the ground; at least three of these to one below the ground. Have at least one leafy vegetable to every one of the pod vegetables.

This chapter gives great ideas on how you can fulfill this wonderful example of eating healthfully and enjoy great flavors at the same time.

When you are planning a get-together and will be serving appetizers and dips, there are so many natural ways to serve them. Fill hollowed-out vegetables such as red, green, or Savoy cabbages and pattypan squashes and pumpkins with your dips, saving the unused vegetable contents for future use. An array of baskets lined with festive paper or linen napkins is a lovely way to present pita chips and crackers as well as raw veggies. Whenever making a cheese tray, I use my large wooden cutting board as a server. When making Asian-inspired hors d'oeuvres, I love to use banana leaves, which you can easily find in an Asian market.

You do not have to spend a lot of money, but do show your guests that they are important to you by creating a beautiful display of food that is made with love just for them. Food should not only be tasty but also draw the eye to its beauty. Trust me! Even the simplest food will taste like gourmet fare if presented in an artistic and creative manner.

When planning an hors d'oeuvres party, I like to have at least four or five different types for guests to nibble on. And then there is the classic wine-and-cheese party, which can be very elegant but actually require much less work.

One rule of thumb for my little gatherings is to set what I call the finish line. You do not want people thinking they can hang out at your house all night. So don't be afraid to say that your entertaining will be ending at a specific time. It will save embarrassment on all fronts. An hors d'oeuvres party is a great way to entertain a group of people when you do not want to cook a full-blown dinner. People always seem to enjoy them.

Such parties can be relaxed and informal for, say, an event on TV; more formal for holidays; or just an occasion for all the neighbors to catch up. You may decide to decorate for the big holidays, in which case I suggest you begin a couple of days ahead of time so as not to be stressed.

Some hors d'oeuvres require cocktail plates or napkins. It can be quite awkward to balance a plate in one hand, a drink in the other, and try to converse with someone and eat at the same time. I have never quite figured out how we are supposed to do that. So try to make the food small enough to eat in one or two bites, and have ample napkins within sight.

The key to great entertaining is to make people feel special and relaxed in your home environment. If you are unused to entertaining, a cocktail party is a great way to start out. The minute guests come in, try to greet them and introduce them to everyone. Of course, if you have fifty people in your home, that is not possible. But do ensure that they are taken care of with a drink and someone to chat with before you take off to attend to your other duties as host. If ever I see someone standing alone, I immediately go to them and try to bring them into a group. I was always taught to do unto others as you would have them do unto you, and I would not want someone feeling neglected!

For some reason, I happen to be one of the most relaxed people in the world when entertaining in my own home. I actually prefer it to going out. I grew up in a family that entertained often, and we all seem to have this gift of not becoming nervous. But if you are nervous, remember that the more you practice, the better you will become at it. I love to plan parties, cook for days if I have to, and invite friends to partake of my efforts. The cocktail party is usually one of the most relaxing to throw. And remember, you don't have to throw a party to make a dip!

Cheese and vegetable trays

Tasty Tuna Pate
Black Bean Hummus
Feta Cheese Dip
Raita
Herbed Soft Cheese Dip
Za'atar Pita Wedges
Chunky Guacamole
Bruschetta
Jennifer's Christmas Eve Cheese Mountain
Canapés
Smoked Salmon Canapé
Feta Cheese Canapés
Grilled Portobello Mushroom Canapés
Asian Pear Canapés
New Potato Skins with Sour Cream
Cheddar Cheese and Marmalade Canapés
Tahini Lemon Dipping Sauce
Vegetarian Pizza
Mango and Black Bean Salsa

While living in Saudi Arabia, most of our social occasions revolved around food. It was not uncommon to have personal chefs from exotic countries like Egypt, India, Thailand, and the Philippines. I was fortunate to have a beautiful and talented woman from Eritrea named "Dahab" (Gold), who taught me many culinary techniques and who also helped me with my two little girls.

Tasty Tuna Pate is an easy-to-make dip she prepared for us. It is creamy and mellow and has been a favorite of my children since they first tasted it. They now make it for their families and friends, and even if people don't *think* they like tuna, they seem to love this. My son-in-law Yann never tires of this dip!

Do keep in mind that tuna should not be eaten by pregnant women, as it does have a high mercury content, and not eaten more frequently than once a week for the rest of us—another special something to indulge in occasionally.

Tasty Tuna Pate
Serves 4-6

2 (6 ounce) cans tuna, drained
5 tablespoons organic unsalted *butter,* room temperature
4 ounces *cream cheese*, room temperature
Cracked black pepper
Lemon slices for garnish
Fresh dill sprigs for garnish

Place tuna, butter, and cream cheese in the bowl of your food processor. Blend until smooth and creamy. Season to taste. Pour into a 4-cup-capacity serving dish and chill for several hours or overnight. Take out of refrigerator 30 minutes before serving; garnish with thin slices of lemon and a few sprigs of fresh dill. Serve with organic veggie slices or whole wheat veggie crackers, or use it as a spread on whole wheat crostini with fresh dill sprigs as a garnish.

Delightful Dips and Hors d'Oeuvres

To me, any hummus is delightful. I was given strict orders by my children and my partner not to include my Middle Eastern garbanzo bean hummus in this book, so I am providing an equally healthful one here. This version is ideal as a vegetarian source of protein. My suggestion is to use freshly squeezed lemon juice, as it truly enhances the flavor of this dip. And there is something about cumin and beans—they seem to love each other.

Serve this dip with brightly hued raw veggies and enjoy!

Black Bean Hummus
Serves 4

2 cloves garlic, minced
1 (15 ounce) can black beans, liquid reserved
2 tablespoons freshly squeezed lemon juice
2 tablespoons tahini
1 teaspoon ground cumin
1/2-1 teaspoon sea salt
1/4 teaspoon cayenne pepper

Place all ingredients in the bowl of your food processor; blend until a buttery mixture; add additional liquid if too thick. Adjust seasoning to taste.

Feta cheese is a virtual staple in most Mediterranean and Middle Eastern homes. This creation is another Saudi Arabian favorite of ours. The choice feta sold in that country, as well as the relatively inexpensive price, meant that it was always in my grocery cart. What a treat to be able to go to the market to buy Bulgarian feta (my favorite) in three-pound blocks or larger.

Feta cheese is a firm, white cheese with a crumbly texture and is made with goat, sheep, or cow's milk. Consider using feta made with either goat or sheep's milk, rather than cow's milk, as it is much easier for the human body to digest. And look for a mild and not overly salty variety.

This dip is so yummy that you'll be asked to make it again and again for family and friends! It's also delicious as a sandwich spread topped with fresh vegetables.

Feta Cheese Dip
Serves 4-6

16 ounces crumbled *feta cheese*
2 cloves garlic, peeled
2 tablespoons extra virgin olive oil
1/2 organic *sweet red, orange,* or *yellow pepper*, chopped
1 *vine-ripened tomato,* diced
1/2 teaspoon cayenne pepper
1/4 pound black Kalamata olives for garnish

Place feta cheese, garlic, and olive oil in the bowl of your food processor; blend until smooth and buttery. Add sweet pepper, tomato, and cayenne; pulse until just blended. Add more olive oil if too thick. Adjust seasoning to taste. Pour into a 4-cup-capacity serving dish; chill for several hours or overnight. Before serving, bring to room temperature. Garnish with Kalamata olives and sprinkle with olive oil.

Serve with organic veggies or toasted whole wheat pita chips to make for a superb start to any meal or to use as a great sandwich spread.

An arrangement of Kalamata
and assorted olives

Delightful Dips and Hors d'Oeuvres

This refreshing concoction is found in Middle Eastern, Mediterranean, and Indian cuisines. It is a great accompaniment to a mezze platter and absolutely delicious served with lamb burgers or chicken za'atar. It is often paired with curries, as well.

Raita
Serves 4

1 cup whole milk *yogurt*
2 cloves garlic, minced
1/2 English cucumber, finely diced
2 chopped spring onions, greens included
1/2 cup chopped fresh mint
1 teaspoon sea salt

Mix ingredients together in a small glass bowl. Cover and refrigerate until ready to use. Will keep for up to 3 days.

Living in Europe for so long, I developed a love for a famous brand of herbed soft cheese. One day, unable to find this delight, I decided to create my own concoction using fresh herbs from the garden. This Herbed Soft Cheese Dip is so simple to put together and is comparable to any store-bought version. The creamy texture just melts in your mouth, and the zing from the garlic, coupled with fresh herbs, makes it come alive. Now I actually prefer my own version to the imported one. I think you will, as well. As always, experiment with this dip and find the herbs you most prefer to make it your own. You are going to be proud when you serve this and say that you created it in your kitchen!

Herbed Soft Cheese Dip
Serves 4-6

8 ounces *cream cheese,* room temperature
1 cup *sour cream* or Greek-style *yogurt* (whole milk)
2 cloves garlic, minced
1/2 cup finely chopped spring onions
1 tablespoon finely chopped fresh thyme or 1 teaspoon dried
1 tablespoon finely chopped, fresh, flat-leaf parsley
1 tablespoon finely chopped fresh marjoram or 1 teaspoon dried
1 teaspoon sea salt
1/2 teaspoon freshly ground black pepper
Sprigs of fresh thyme for garnish
Edible flowers for garnish (optional)

Place cream cheese, sour cream or yogurt, garlic, and spring onions in the bowl of your food processor. Pulse 10 to 12 times, until just blended. Add fresh herbs, sea salt, and pepper and pour into a 4-cup-capacity serving dish. Adjust seasoning to taste. Serve at room temperature with organic veggies, toasted whole wheat pita chips, or toasted rye bread to make for a superb snack and dip.

If desired, add sprigs of fresh thyme or organic edible flowers on top of the dip to create an aesthetic appeal.

Owning a sailboat at one point in my life was quite an experience. To be repeated? Never! On weekends, we would spend our time on the Red Sea and sail to one of the hundreds of spectacular coral reefs, sometimes 10 to 15 miles out. There would always be schools of dolphins following us and flying through the air, which would make my girls scream with delight. Actually, me too! The water is the color of turquoise and also very warm, which makes for superb scuba diving. The myriad of fish and sea life was like something I have never seen since, and I have such fond memories of those balmy days.

We always had these homemade pita chips on hand for snacks and for those who suffered from seasickness—they just seemed to be a diet staple for seafarers. And we actually did sail across the Red Sea to Sudan on a friend's rather large yacht, to dive with hammerhead sharks in a Jacques Cousteau reserve. On the way over, we ran into one of the scariest storms, making even the captain and crew ill. Once out of the storm, a very battered and sorry-looking group we were. The only thing any of us could stomach was these life-savers!

Za'atar is the star in this recipe. It is an *Arabic* term referring to any various local herbs of the *mint family*, including *marjoram, oregano,* and *thyme*. I love to sprinkle it on *hummus* or serve it with olive oil as a superb dip. Za'atar is frequently added to white cheeses, such as haloumi, which is another Middle Eastern delight, and grilled or served chilled. It is also used to spice meats and vegetables. Actually, once you start eating this combination of herbs, you will find a zillion different ways to use it. It can be found in Middle Eastern shops or ordered from mail-order Web sites. But it is also very simple to make your own (see *Herbs and Edible Flowers*, page xix).

Always buy whole wheat pita bread, as it is nutritionally preferable to the white variety. Also, the flavor of whole wheat is so much better!

Za'atar Pita Wedges
Serves 6-8

2 small whole wheat pita rounds
2 tablespoons extra virgin olive oil
2 tablespoons za'atar

Preheat oven to 300°. Fold pita bread in half, and cut down the middle with clean kitchen scissors; cut into 4-inch triangles.

In a medium mixing bowl, mix the olive oil and za'atar; add the pita triangles and toss to coat. Spread the pita triangles in an even layer on a rimmed baking sheet; bake, stirring occasionally, until golden, 12 to 15 minutes.

The pita chips can be stored in a cookie tin for a week or frozen in an airtight bag for up to three months.

Guacamole is a great way for everyone to eat avocados. This dish is always featured in Mexican restaurants, and now it is a staple dip at most parties. Unfortunately, many versions are either overprocessed, resulting in a listless puree with no texture, or there are too many seasonings, making for a fiery encounter.

This version is chunky and not perfectly smooth. You will be able to taste the rich and nutty flavor of the avocado fruit, along with hints of acid from the fresh lime juice. For children, I suggest omitting the jalapeño chile. I add hard-boiled eggs in this recipe, which gives even more consistency, but you can omit this item, if you like.

When I serve this dip, I try to use a festive pottery bowl, to highlight the Mexican culture, and then garnish it with 3-inch long slivers of sweet yellow, red, and orange peppers, making a circular decoration around the rim of the bowl. Place the avocado pit in the middle of the dip to prevent any discoloration, and voila!—it resembles the shape of a sunflower and makes for a great eye-catcher.

Chunky Guacamole
Serves 6-8

1-2 tablespoons minced garlic
2 tablespoons minced onion
1 small jalapeño chili, seeded and finely minced
1 small tomato, seeded and diced
1/4 cup chopped fresh cilantro leaves
1/4 teaspoon ground cumin
1/2 teaspoon sea salt
3 medium Haas avocados, ripened
2 hard-boiled eggs (optional)
4 tablespoons fresh lime juice

Place the garlic, onion, jalapeño chili, tomato, cilantro, cumin, and sea salt in a medium-size bowl. Pit and scoop out the flesh of one avocado; mash lightly with the hard-boiled eggs (if using) and add to bowl. Reserve the pit and set aside. Pit the two remaining avocados; cut flesh into medium-size cubes; add to bowl. Do not overmix or you will lose the chunky texture desired. Sprinkle lime juice over avocado mixture. Adjust seasoning, if needed. Spoon into a serving dish and decorate as explained above, if desired.

If not serving immediately, the guacamole can be covered with plastic wrap and refrigerated for up to one day. (Make sure plastic wrap is pressed directly onto the surface of the dip, or it will turn brown.)

Delightful Dips and Hors d'Oeuvres

Bruschetta is definitely a summer dish, for a time when tomatoes and basil are bursting with flavor and are readily available in your garden or local farmers market. What memory could be better than sitting in an outdoor ristorante on Lake Garda (in the famous Lake District of northern Italy), sipping a glass of white wine, and eating these messy delights with my whole clan. My daughter Brooke was married near the Garden Lake. Every time I make these, my mind wanders back to that area of the world where people just seem to live life to the fullest. They take such pride in their cooking, and eating is not a necessity, it is a way of life! Meals can last for hours as family and friends converse.

In just about any home or restaurant you visit in Italy, you are likely to be served this fabulous appetizer. Most recipes call for balsamic vinegar, but I have substituted freshly squeezed lemon juice for a more refreshing and healthy alternative. But choose either version to suit your taste.

Note: I do not suggest using canned tomatoes, as they will be too soggy for this recipe. If you cannot find Roma tomatoes, use a sweet variety instead.

Bruschetta
Serves 6-8

8 medium (about 1 pound) *vine-ripened Roma tomatoes*
8 fresh basil leaves, chopped
2 cloves garlic, minced
1/2 medium red onion, minced
1/4 cup lemon juice
1/4 cup extra virgin olive oil plus extra to toast crostini
Sea salt
Freshly ground black pepper
Handful of fresh basil leaves for garnish

Crostini
1 whole wheat baguette or rustic bread, cut into 1/2-inch slices on the diagonal
1 clove garlic, peeled, sliced in half
1 tablespoon extra virgin olive oil for topping
Fresh basil leaves for garnish

Prepare the tomatoes first by removing the skins. I do this by placing them in a medium-size mixing bowl and pouring boiling water over them. Once the skins start to blister (usually one minute), take them out with tongs and peel off the skin. Cut tomatoes in half and remove seeds; cut into 1/2-inch dice; place in a medium-size bowl.

In a small, separate bowl, mix basil, garlic, red onion, lemon juice, olive oil, sea salt, and cracked pepper. Pour mixture over the tomatoes; stir. Let the mixture sit while you prepare crostini.

First, brush both sides of the bread with olive oil. Grill on your barbeque, or place on a baking sheet and broil in the oven. The important thing is that the bread gets golden brown on both sides. Once bread is toasted but still warm, rub one side with garlic slice. Place on serving platter, and just before guests arrive, put a heaping tablespoon of tomatoes on top and drizzle with olive oil. Do not make this too far in advance, as the bread will become soggy. Garnish with fresh basil leaves.

Brooke, Lake Garda, Italy

Every Christmas Eve, my sister Jennifer and her large family have an open house in their beautiful home in New Brunswick, Canada. We grew up in a village named Rothesay (pronounced Ros-say), after the one in northern Scotland. There are many traditions carried out to this day in our little northern haven. For this occasion, my brother-in-law Chas and nephews Hugh, Sam, and Joe proudly wear their Mackay tartan kilts. Other friends (male and female) wear their family tartans as well. Often someone plays bagpipes, which moves me to tears and sends shivers up my spine.

There is always an opulent choice of local seafood, crudités, Virginia peanuts, Jennifer's homemade breads and rolls, fresh fruit, freshly baked sweets, and Jennifer's famous giant cheese mountain, which weighs a small ton.

As there are normally 75 to 100 people at this gathering, you can imagine the challenge of downsizing this recipe for a small group of 8 to 10 people. But I have given it my best effort. However, if you want to make a larger batch for future parties—or save some of this one—it can be frozen. You're going to love this cheese mountain and so are your friends. There are cheese balls, and then there is this majestic mountain inspired by my older sister!

Note: If you are not a nut lover or are allergic to nuts, my suggestion would be to cover the cheese mountain with dried cranberries, dried blueberries, or dried cherries. Or you may wish to divide the mixture in half, depending on the number of guests, and make one with nuts and one with dried fruits.

Jennifer's Christmas Eve Cheese Mountain
Serves 10

2 cups chopped walnuts or pecans
1 teaspoon maple syrup
1/2 tablespoon cayenne pepper
1/2 teaspoon sea salt
1 cup grated *cheddar cheese*
1 cup grated *Gruyere cheese*
1/2 cup crumbled *blue cheese*
1 cup grated *Gouda cheese*
1 cup *Brie,* room temperature
1 cup *Camembert,* room temperature
1/2 cup *ricotta cheese*
1/4 cup port or sherry (optional)
2 cloves garlic, minced
2 teaspoons dry mustard
2 teaspoons Worcestershire sauce

Preheat oven to 300°. Mix nuts with maple syrup, cayenne pepper, and sea salt. Place on a baking sheet; bake in preheated oven for 10 minutes. Set aside.

Place remaining ingredients in your food processor and mix until smooth. Remove cheese mixture and form into the shape of a mountain, the base larger than the top. Be creative and get your family involved in this one. Cover the mountain with toasted nuts. Wrap with several layers of clear plastic and refrigerate for several hours. Remove from refrigerator 30 minutes before serving. Serve with whole wheat crackers.

Delightful Dips and Hors d'Oeuvres

Canapés

I love knowing the derivation of words. Canapé is French for "couch." This term was adopted because the toppings sit atop a piece of bread as if sitting on little sofas. These are great to serve at parties and should be small enough to eat in one or two bites. They are the ultimate finger food. Now canapés are no longer just pieces of toasted bread—polenta, filo pastry, and small tarts fall under this category as well.

If using bread as the base for your canapés, remove the crusts and use cookie cutters to form various shapes. You can toast your bread or not, but I like the crunch and it will prevent the bread from getting soggy after the toppings are added. Also, you can make your canapés in advance and store them in a cookie tin for several days until needed. Once you have cut them into shapes, place your canapés on a cookie sheet and bake in a 300° oven until toasted on both sides.

This is a colorful, savory, uncomplicated combination and relatively painless to make. Most people will be thrilled to bite into a piece of the ocean, knowing that they are getting their Omega 3s. Rye bread canapés are a great complement to this topping.

Smoked Salmon Canapés
Serves 8

1/2 cup *sour cream*
1 tablespoon mayonnaise
1 teaspoon lemon juice
Sea salt
Freshly ground black pepper
4 ounces smoked salmon
Lemon slices for garnish
Fresh dill for garnish
Canapés

Stir the sour cream, mayonnaise, lemon juice, and seasoning together until well combined. Spoon a teaspoonful onto each canapé. Top with a piece of smoked salmon. Garnish with a sprig of fresh dill and a sliver of lemon.

These canapés remind me of sunny days sailing in the Greek Isles or, more realistically, a gathering of friends in my garden in Virginia on a summer day. My dear friend Silvio has two grandsons, Georges and Pierre, who actually visit the island of Kalamata every summer, where their dad has olive orchards. I have a secret love affair with olives, so I would probably be in trouble if left alone in that area!

Fresh, vine-ripened tomatoes can easily replace the sun-dried variety when available. There is an intense flavor to this concoction, and the contrast in colors is exciting. I suggest using whole wheat canapés for this combination.

Feta Cheese Canapés
Serves 8

1 cup *Feta Cheese* Dip (page 6), room temperature
1/4 cup drained and chopped *sun-dried tomatoes* or 2 large *vine-ripened tomatoes*, diced
10 pitted Kalamata olives, sliced
Canapés

If using fresh tomatoes, season with sea salt and pepper; let drain for several minutes. Spread canapés with a thin layer of feta cheese spread. Place tomatoes on top and garnish with an olive slice.

Delightful Dips and Hors d'Oeuvres

I love the earthiness of this combination. There is a great contrast in texture: the spinach gives a crunchy texture to the velvety smooth texture of Portobello mushrooms and goat cheese. The nuttiness of walnut oil also complements the Portobello mushrooms, but olive oil is equally as pleasing. You can use the aid of cookie cutters to cut the polenta into desired shapes!

Grilled Portobello Mushroom Canapés
Serves 8-10

2 cups vegetable stock
1 cup instant polenta plus extra for dusting
2 tablespoons walnut oil or olive oil, divided, plus extra for brushing
1 tablespoon red onion, minced
1 teaspoon garlic, minced
1 tablespoon parsley, chopped
4 large Portobello mushrooms, diced
4 ounces *goat cheese,* room temperature
1 tablespoon *sour cream*
1 cup baby organic *spinach* leaves

Lightly grease a rectangular cookie sheet; line with unbleached parchment paper. In a large pan, bring stock to a boil; reduce heat and add 1 cup polenta. Cook for 10 to 15 minutes, stirring constantly until it becomes like porridge. Spread onto cookie sheet and refrigerate until firm, approximately 30 minutes. Cut into desired shapes and place on prepared cookie sheet. Brush with a bit of oil and dust with extra polenta. Bake approximately 10 minutes, until the polenta is golden brown.

Heat 1 tablespoon of oil in a medium-size sauté pan over medium-high heat; add onion, garlic, parsley, and mushrooms. Cook for 4 to 5 minutes, stirring occasionally. Meanwhile, mix together goat cheese, sour cream, and 1 tablespoon oil to form a silky paste.

Spread cheese mixture onto polenta canapés. Top with spinach leaf, then the mushroom mixture.

The base of this canapé is actually a slice of one of my favorite pears—Asian. They are round and crunchy, with a delicious taste, and can be found in Asian markets or most grocery stores. Gorgonzola is a creamy Italian cheese of the blue cheese family and is also easy to find in most grocery stores. However, if it is not obtainable, substitute blue cheese. We produce a superb variety in the United States called Maytag. You can buy candied walnuts, but making them is easy. There is such dimension to this fruity canapé.

Asian Pear Canapés
Serves 10-12

2 Asian *pears* (about 1 pound), cut into 1/2 -inch-thick slices
5 ounces sliced *Gorgonzola cheese,* room temperature
1 tablespoon *butter,* melted
1 tablespoon maple syrup
1/3 cup walnuts

First, prepare the candied walnuts. Preheat oven to 300°. Line baking sheet with unbleached parchment paper. Mix together maple syrup and butter in a small mixing bowl. Add whole walnuts to coat. Spread out nut mixture on baking sheet and bake for 10 to 12 minutes, until crunchy. Let cool. Top pear slices with Gorgonzola and garnish with candied walnuts.

Oh, what a treat to make these for your guests! Don't count on there being any left after the party, either. I love these during early summer, when the first new potatoes arrive. Potatoes are one of those vegetables that should be eaten only if organic.

The filled potato skins can be made in advance and refrigerated. Grill them just before your guests arrive. These will melt in your mouth!

My good friend Susie Burke taught me to make "spuds" the Irish way—she is from Belfast. First, rub the cleaned potatoes in oil, followed by the sea salt, and then bake. This gives an extra crunch to them. Of course, you can omit the sea salt step.

New Potato Skins with Sour Cream
Serves 10–12

30 small new *potatoes*, halved
2 tablespoons sunflower oil
1 tablespoon coarse sea salt
10 ounces *sour cream*
4 ounces sharp *cheddar cheese,* grated
Finely chopped rosemary for garnish

Preheat oven to 400°. Line a baking sheet with unbleached parchment paper. Place potatoes on prepared baking sheet; bake for 30 minutes, or until cooked through. When cool enough, spoon out the flesh, leaving a 1/4-inch border; discard flesh. Return potatoes to baking sheet and bake for another 30 minutes, or until crisp.

In the meantime, combine the sour cream and grated cheddar. Fill crisp potato skins with cheese mixture; broil on baking sheet for 2 minutes. Place on a serving plate and garnish with rosemary.

Okay, I just had to put in this old-fashioned recipe because my mum always made these "back in the day." Actually, I think everyone in our village made these. I used to gobble them up. They are very easy to make and easy to love. Make some with bacon and some without for your vegetarian friends.

**Cheddar Cheese and Marmalade Canapés
Serves 10**

10 slices whole wheat bread, cut into squares
3-4 tablespoons orange marmalade
5 ounces sharp *cheddar cheese,* thinly sliced
5 *bacon strips,* cut into 3-inch strips, partially cooked

Preheat oven to 400°. Toast one side of bread before assembling. Spread a small portion of marmalade on pre-toasted bread. Add a square of cheese smaller than the piece of bread and top with bacon (if using). Place on baking sheet and cook until bacon is crisp and cheese is melted. Serve warm.

Delightful Dips and Hors d'Oeuvres

If you have the chance to travel to the Middle East, you will likely be served this dipping sauce in homes and restaurants. It is simple, healthy, and absolutely refreshing served with a tray of raw vegetables or toasted pita wedges.

It can also be used as a spread for a superb vegetarian sandwich, using whole wheat pita and a filling of grated carrots, sliced tomatoes, cucumbers, feta cheese, and black olives.

Tahini Lemon Dipping Sauce
Serves 4

1/2 cup tahini
1/2 cup Greek-style *yogurt* or whole milk *yogurt*
Juice and zest of 1 lemon
Pinch of cayenne (optional)

In a small bowl, mix ingredients together until well blended. Add a pinch of cayenne pepper, if desired. If dip is too thick, use water to thin.

Me, in Marrakech, Morocco

I recently visited Toronto, where I lived in the 70s. It has always been a great city to me, but I was amazed at how clean and how many great restaurants there are serving healthy and eclectic food—it has become one of North America's top culinary destinations. One night, while roaming the many charming streets, I was thrilled to find a cute bistro with great, and I mean great, pizzas. They were not only served on whole wheat crust, but *thin* whole wheat crust. Pizza heaven to me! When I returned home, I started making pizzas for parties, but *my* way, with a variety of vegetables. They became quite a hit. I do feel that by making your own sauce, you will enhance the taste. Now that whole wheat pizza dough is readily available in many stores, much time can be saved. Use any combination of vegetables you like. If buffalo mozzarella is not available, use a good quality, whole milk variety.

Oddly enough, this pizza is also delicious served cold. Add a composed salad and you have a great lunch.

For this recipe, a large rectangular baking sheet is recommended.

Vegetarian Pizza
Serves 10-12 people

Flour for rolling dough
1 pound whole wheat pizza dough
2 tablespoons grated Parmesan

For the sauce
2 tablespoons extra virgin olive oil
1 medium white onion, diced
2 cloves garlic, minced
5 tablespoons tomato paste
1 cup water
Sea salt
Freshly ground black pepper

For the topping
1 large ball (8 ounces) buffalo milk mozzarella, thinly sliced
2 cups grated Parmesan
2 medium white onions, thinly sliced
1 medium-size sweet red pepper, thinly sliced
2 cups sliced button mushrooms
2 cups thinly sliced zucchini
2 medium Roma tomatoes, sliced
1 tablespoon dried oregano

Preheat oven to 400°. Roll dough on a floured work surface into a rectangular shape to fit the baking sheet. Sprinkle with 2 tablespoons grated Parmesan. Place in freezer while you make the tomato sauce and prep veggies.

To make the sauce, heat olive oil in a medium-size saucepan over medium heat. Add onion and garlic; cook until translucent. Add tomato paste, water, sea salt, and pepper. Continue to cook over medium heat, stirring occasionally, until the consistency of a thick paste. Cool to room temperature.

Remove pizza dough from freezer. Pour sauce evenly over dough. Top with mozzarella and Parmesan, then remaining veggies and oregano. Bake for approximately 20 minutes.

Let cool for several minutes before cutting into bite-size squares.

Delightful Dips and Hors d'Oeuvres

This refreshing dip has a Latin American flavor as well as a Middle Eastern touch and can be made as spicy as you like. It is also very healthy and is fabulous served with organic spicy-or-not taco chips. I also like to put freshly cut lime wedges around the bowl for added color. Try using a cheery-looking serving bowl with this salsa. It is also an excellent side dish to accompany grilled tuna steaks, fish, or chicken.

Mango and Black Bean Salsa
Serves 4-6

1 (15 ounce) can black beans
1 medium mango, peeled, pitted, and cut into 1/2-inch dice
1/2 cup finely diced *red bell pepper*
1/2 cup finely diced *green bell pepper*
1/4 cup minced red onion
1 small jalapeño pepper, seeded and finely diced
1 cup chopped fresh cilantro
1/2 cup lime juice (about 3-4 limes)
3 tablespoons extra virgin olive oil
2 teaspoons ground cumin
1 teaspoon sea salt

Put all ingredients together in a mixing bowl to blend. Adjust seasoning to taste. Put in a plastic container and refrigerate for several hours so flavors can marry. Serve at room temperature. This can be refrigerated for up to 4 days. Serve with organic corn chips.

Salads in the Raw and Not So Raw

With today's health conscious population, the consumption of a midday salad has become the norm. Salads help keep your body alkaline, which in turn helps build your immune system and prevent colds and flu. Here is Cayce's take on this:

(Q) Should plenty of lettuce be eaten?
(A) Plenty of lettuce should always be eaten by most *every* body, for this supplies an effluvium in the blood stream itself that is a destructive force to *most* of those influences that attack the blood stream. It's a purifier.   **404-6**

No modern-day nutritionist could say it any better. In fact, Cayce said that at least one meal a day should consist of totally raw vegetables. Alternatively, a salad should be included with the lunch and dinner meals.

Surviving on earth without the daily consumption of fresh salad is not an option for me. I absolutely adore salads, whether composed of an abundance of in-season vegetables or fresh fruit. I have rarely bought salad in a bag, as I want it to be as fresh as possible, but it can be a godsend when short on time. The point is simply to make sure you eat lots of greens and green, leafy vegetables!

During World Wars I and II, an initiative was put forth in the United States, Canada, and the United Kingdom to plant what were coined "victory gardens." In an effort to reduce pressure on the public food supply, citizens started planting vegetable, herb, and fruit gardens on their lawns, in vacant lots, and on apartment-building rooftops. People were encouraged to can and preserve their vegetables to allow for commercial food to be sent to the troops overseas. Subsequently, there were over 20 million victory gardens planted in the United States alone. Neighborhoods put their produce together to form co-operatives.

There is renewed interest in victory gardens, with many Web sites offering advice on how to plant from seed. If every person planted some form of garden, just as in days gone by, I feel there would be rewards on many levels. And with the average person currently feeling a pocketbook pinch, such a task may help to offset this burden. Small vegetable or herb gardens can be planted whether you live in an apartment or a house. Windowsills are ideal and decorative places for planting fresh herbs. Large pots can house tomatoes, lettuce, peppers, and other veggies easily and can be placed outside your front step. Another money saver is to buy from local farmers or to join a CSA (community supported agriculture).

Every country has its own version of salads. In this section, the ones I learned to love in my travels are included. And then there are others that have been created or recreated from classic recipes. As always, use your imagination to make your very own invention!

In Europe, the composed salad is popular. This is basically a layer of lettuce topped with a variety of ingredients tossed in together or laid out in rows to create an aesthetic plate. You can create a seafood salad, a fruit salad, a raw or cooked vegetable salad, or a salad with a bevy of freshly cut herbs. By adding walnuts, pine nuts, or almonds, you will achieve a crunchier texture. Sunflower, sesame, and pumpkin seeds are a fabulous way to add more protein, as well.

TOASTING NUTS AND SEEDS

Toasting the nuts or seeds will enhance their flavor and add a greater depth to the salad or featured recipe. Heartier nuts and larger quantities of seeds can be toasted in a preheated 350° oven:

Spread nuts or seeds on a cookie sheet and bake for about 7 to 10 minutes, depending on size and quantity, until aromatic and lightly browned. Remove from oven and cool.

Pine nuts need to be baked at a lower oven temperature—300°—just long enough to turn a caramel color. If they are overcooked, they will have a bitter taste.

More delicate seeds or smaller quantities of nuts can be toasted in a dry skillet over medium-low- to medium-high heat for just a few minutes, then cooled. Sesame seeds especially need to be watched carefully; once they release their toasty scent, remove them immediately from the pan to cool.

Dried cranberries and raisins give a natural sweetness to certain salads and lend their own nutritional virtues.

As with all whole foods, choose only the freshest locally grown and seasonal ingredients possible. Oh, what joy in the summertime to have a harvest of vine-ripened tomatoes picked at their peak. The possibilities are endless when it comes to composing salads. Even in the autumn or winter months, there are numerous possibilities with seasonal veggies and fruits. Do ensure that you thoroughly wash all vegetables and fruits before eating, to avoid any food-borne illness.

More elegant salads can be served as an entrée for a special dinner. In the summer months, everyone enjoys a fresh salad at lunchtime. And in the evening, a light salad with fresh herbs is great to accompany your meal. The importance of introducing children to salads at a young age cannot be overemphasized. There is no reason why they will not like them if you give them the opportunity. When I was growing up, salads were a staple at mealtime in my family, and this healthy habit has been passed down to my children and grandchildren.

Naturally, most people have their own favorite salad dressings and may not eat raw veggies without them. If that is what it takes to get one to eat greens, then that is fine. Cayce highly recommended the use of olive oil as a dressing and often a mayonnaise dressing, which is such an easy condiment to make. He also suggested lemon juice at times and favored "pure" wine vinegar if any vinegar was to be used. To enhance the flavors of the various salads, a great variety of healthy and easy-to-make vinaigrettes and dressings are included in the next section.

When using fresh lettuce, wash it well and ensure that the leaves are dry. Definitely invest in a salad spinner, as it will make your life much easier. Who is not into simplicity these days? This way, the leaves are well dried and you will also save money on paper towels, which means ecological savings. Children love to help in the kitchen, and spinning lettuce is a chore that appeals to them.

Listed below are some common salad greens, but by no means limit yourself to these alone.

Arugula (Rocket)—Commonly found in Italy and becoming popular here, served with shaved Parmesan cheese. It has an almost bitter taste.

Bibb Butter head—Delicate and sweet-tasting.

Belgian endive—Slightly bitter-tasting and most commonly served with toasted walnuts and blue cheese dressing.

Dandelion greens—The young leaves are used for salad greens and have a slightly bitter taste.

Escarole—Has a slightly bitter taste and can be eaten raw or cooked. Great cut into thin strips and added to vegetable soup.

Frisee (curly endive)—Frisee means "curly" in French. This has a slightly bitter or nutty flavor and is popular served with Gruyere cheese, roasted beets, and toasted walnuts.

Lolla Rossa—Deeply curled, loose-leaf variety that has magenta-red edges. Adds great color to any salad mixture.

Red or Green Leafy Lettuce—Delicate loose-leaf variety with a sweet taste.

Romaine—A hearty lettuce and a must in Caesar salads.

Spring Mix (Muscelin Greens)—This has become one of North America's favorite ways to eat salad. Sweet and colorful, but fragile.

Watercress—Has a peppery taste and is great as a salad green or garnish.

Herbed Quinoa Salad
Winter Fruits and Nuts Quinoa Salad
Summer Fruit Quinoa Salad
Broccoli and Sunflower Seed Salad
Southern Sweet Potato Salad
Wild Rice Salad
Tomato and Mozzarella Stack
Toasted Goat Cheese Salad
Feta and Watermelon Salad
Wilderness Mango Salad
Middle Eastern Tabouleh
Fatima's Fatoush Salad
Rhodes Island Greek Salad
Caesar Salad
Moroccan Carrot Salad
Salade Nicoise
Celestial Chicken Salad
Lou Lou's Lunar Tunar Salad
Sesame Noodle Salad
Lime Gelatin with Grated Vegetables
Very Berry Lime Gelatin Salad
Raw Beet and Orange Salad
Shaved Fennel and Beet Salad
Bree's Virginia Beach Summer Salad
Asian Slaw
Curried Couscous and Chicken Salad
Sienna's Summer Salad
Exotic Fresh Fruit Salad

Quinoa (pronounced keen-wah) is an ancient grain. It has a delicious nutty flavor and texture. The Incas referred to it as the "Mother Grain," as it was a main staple in their diet. Quinoa is a complete protein, meaning that it supplies all the nine essential amino acids. For that reason, it is an excellent choice for vegans and those who are concerned about adequate protein intake. Quinoa is fast becoming a staple in health conscious diets. It is prepared in the same manner as rice, and like rice, it is gluten-free. When I first started buying quinoa, it was only available in health food stores, but it is now stocked in many grocery stores. If it is not available, ask your grocer to stock it for you.

Toasting pine nuts for the recipe will bring out their natural, buttery flavor, and your guests and family will appreciate your effort.

Herbed Quinoa Salad
Serves 4

2 cups water or vegetable stock
1 cup organic quinoa
1 cup finely chopped flat-leaf parsley
1 cup finely chopped fresh basil
1/2 cup pine nuts, toasted
3 tablespoons Bree's Citrus Vinaigrette (page 59)

In a medium saucepan, bring the water or vegetable stock to a boil; add quinoa. Cover and simmer for approximately 15 minutes. Meanwhile, toast pine nuts in a cast-iron or heavy skillet over medium-high heat, shaking often until they turn golden brown; cool. Transfer cooked quinoa to a medium mixing bowl and let cool. Add fresh herbs and pine nuts. Top with vinaigrette and mix well. Cover and refrigerate until ready to serve.

Salads in the Raw and Not So Raw

Quinoa is light, easy to digest, and versatile, lending itself so beautifully to fresh fruit to create a salad. Here are two examples, using fruits from both winter and summer seasons, respectively. Both of these delightful salads are great served with grilled fish or chicken or atop green leafy lettuce.

Winter Fruits and Nuts Quinoa Salad
Serves 4

2 cups water
1 cup quinoa
2 navel oranges, peeled and sectioned, juices reserved
Seeds from 1 pomegranate, juices reserved
1/4 cup pumpkin seeds
1/2 cup raisins
1/4 cup toasted walnuts
1 teaspoon cinnamon

In a medium saucepan, bring water to a boil; add quinoa. Cover and simmer for approximately 15 minutes. Transfer to a medium-size mixing bowl; cool to room temperature. Add fruit, juices, seeds, raisins, and cinnamon and mix well. Cover and refrigerate until ready to serve.

Summer Fruit Quinoa Salad
Serves 4

2 cups water
1 cup quinoa
2 peaches, peeled, pit removed, and diced into 1/2-inch cubes, juices reserved
2 plums, pit removed, and diced into 1/2-inch cubes, juices reserved
1/4 cup finely chopped fresh mint

In a medium saucepan, bring water to a boil; add quinoa. Cover and simmer for approximately 15 minutes. Transfer to a medium-size mixing bowl; cool to room temperature. Add fruit, juices, and mint and mix well. Cover and refrigerate until ready to serve.

My sister Jennifer sent me this recipe, which combines a number of sweet and savory ingredients that will complement any salad buffet. Her recipe calls for white sugar, but may I suggest one tablespoon beet sugar or local honey. This healthy salad is absolutely yummy and a superb way to introduce children to raw broccoli and new flavors.

Broccoli and Sunflower Seed Salad
Serves 4

1 cup *sour cream* or Greek-style *yogurt*
2 tablespoons mayonnaise
1 tablespoon beet sugar or honey
2 tablespoons lemon zest
2 cups broccoli florets
8 ounces *feta cheese,* crumbled
1/2 cup unsulphured raisins
1/2 cup salted sunflower seeds
1/4 cup finely minced red onion (optional)

In a medium bowl, mix sour cream, mayonnaise, sugar or honey, and lemon zest. Stir in broccoli, feta, raisins, sunflower seeds, and onion; cover and refrigerate until ready to serve.

Living in the South, sweet potatoes are a staple in our diet. Remember Bubba in Forrest Gump? Southerners have so many uses for sweet potatoes that one could write a book. One day, I decided to perhaps create a healthier version of the classic white potato salad, using sweet potatoes instead. This potato salad has now become a favorite of mine, and I really don't miss the other one at all. It is a great picnic or cookout salad and goes well with just about anything. I like to leave the skins on for nutritive value, but make sure you scrub them well before cooking.

Southern Sweet Potato Salad
Serves 4

1 pound fresh sweet *potatoes*, diced into 1-inch cubes
1 cup toasted walnuts
2 *celery* stalks, diced
1/2 cup dried cranberries
4 tablespoons balsamic vinaigrette (page 58)

Preheat oven to 400°. Cook sweet potatoes in a medium pot for approximately 10 minutes, until just tender; do not overcook. Strain and place in medium mixing bowl; allow to cool.

Meanwhile, spread walnuts on a cookie sheet and bake in preheated 350° oven for 7-10 minutes. Or toast walnuts in a skillet over medium-high heat for 5 to 7 minutes. Cool nuts; add to sweet potatoes. Add celery and cranberries to mixture. Carefully mix in balsamic vinaigrette, careful not to break up potatoes. Cover and refrigerate for several hours before serving.

Wild rice is grown in fresh water and is actually a grain. It has a nutty flavor, and mixed with dried cranberries, freshly chopped parsley, and citrus vinaigrette, it makes for an elegant side salad. There are many virtues to this salad. Rice is gluten-free so it is great for people who are allergic to wheat and other grains containing gluten. And, of course, this salad is much healthier than the normal white rice salad. It has a magnificent crunch to it, as well.

Wild Rice Salad
Serves 4

1 cup wild rice
3 cups vegetable broth or water
1/2 cup dried cranberries
Bunch of flat-leaf parsley, chopped
3 *celery stalks,* chopped into 1/2-inch dice
1/2 cup toasted walnuts (optional)
1/4 cup Bree's Citrus Vinaigrette (page 59)

Rinse wild rice and place in medium saucepan with vegetable broth or water; stir. Cover and simmer until rice is tender, about 50 minutes. Place in a medium bowl and let cool.

Add cranberries, parsley, celery, and walnuts, if using. Toss with vinaigrette. Refrigerate for at least one hour or until ready to serve.

This is best served as a first course or for lunch, with a crunchy whole wheat baguette. My kids and I love to eat this sensational and easy-to-make salad on a summer day when tomatoes are plump and juicy. If you cannot find buffalo milk mozzarella, do inquire about it; the deli section of your store just may have it. But be sure to use a good quality mozzarella if the buffalo milk variety is unavailable. Avocados are such a delicacy and have a silky texture. The colors of this combination will remind you of the Italian flag.

Tomato and Mozzarella Stack
Serves 4

1 small red onion, thinly sliced
1/4 cup Bree's Citrus Vinaigrette (page 59) or Balsamic Vinaigrette (page 58)
2 medium Haas avocados
2 large vine-ripened *tomatoes*
2 balls buffalo milk *mozzarella* (about 10 ounces total)
8 large fresh basil leaves for garnish, rinsed and patted dry

In a small bowl, marinate red onion in your choice of vinaigrette dressing; this will render the onions sweeter. Cut avocados into halves; remove pits and peel skin. Starting at the top of each avocado, slice into 1/4-inch, half-moon slices. Remove stem from tomatoes. Do not cut tomatoes in half; rather, slice into 1/4-inch-thick rounds. Slice mozzarella into 1/4-inch rounds. Stack basil leaves and roll as you would to make a cigar. Slice into thin strips.

On individual serving plates, stack one tomato slice, one avocado slice, and one mozzarella slice. Repeat. Surround stacks with sliced onions, and drizzle onions with remaining vinaigrette. Garnish with basil strips.

This is really a delightful salad and simply made. It is called Salade au Chevre Chaud in France and is always featured on restaurant menus there. The goat cheese melts in your mouth, and the simplicity of this salad makes for an easy first course or luncheon meal. I cannot tell you how often my family and I have eaten this salad at home. We are all addicted.

Note: To make Dijon mustard vinaigrette, follow the recipe for Bree's Citrus Vinaigrette (page 59) and whisk in 1 tablespoon good quality Dijon mustard until well blended.

Toasted Goat Cheese Salad
Serves 4

4 cups *muscelin greens (spring mix)*
8-ounce *goat cheese* log, cut into 4 equal rounds
4 slices whole wheat baguette or 4 baguette-size slices of hearty grain bread
4 tablespoons Dijon mustard vinaigrette (see note above)

Place one round of goat cheese on each piece of bread. Broil in oven until cheese melts slightly. Place one cup of field greens on each serving plate; top with goat cheese toasts. Drizzle greens with the Dijon mustard citrus vinaigrette.

We are lucky in Virginia, as melons of all sorts grow at our local farms. Every year, I anxiously await this most favored fruit of mine. I saw a version of this salad in a magazine a couple of years ago. Feta with watermelon may sound unusual, but it is actually a cool combo. The natural sweetness of watermelon is accentuated by the sea salt in feta cheese and black olives. Try using Kalamata or other good quality olives rather than canned ones—you will taste the difference immediately. I would also suggest buying a mini seedless watermelon. Once the watermelon is cut in half and the pulp removed, both sides of the shell can be used as a serving vessel. This makes for a festive centerpiece on your picnic table.

Feta and Watermelon Salad
Serves 6-8

1 medium-size red onion (optional)
Juice of 2-3 limes
1 mini seedless watermelon (about 3 pounds)
8 ounces *feta cheese*
Small bunch flat-leaf parsley, roughly chopped
Small bunch fresh mint, roughly chopped
1/4 cup (2 ounces) pitted black olives
2 tablespoons extra virgin olive oil
Cracked black pepper

Peel onion and cut in half; cut into thin half moons. Place in a small bowl; pour lime juice over onions and let sit while assembling other ingredients. (This takes the sharpness out of the onions.)

Cut watermelon in half; scoop out fruit, leaving a 3-inch border. Cut watermelon into 1-inch cubes or triangles. Cut feta cheese the same size. Place watermelon and feta in a large mixing bowl. Add rest of ingredients, including lime juice; mix gently. Season with cracked black pepper to taste.

While visiting Wilderness, South Africa, my youngest daughter, Bree, and granddaughter Anais enjoyed this salad immensely. This is their interpretation of one of my favorite salads, which can be eaten any time of the year. What really sets this salad apart are the fresh herbs. The blend of flavors all but burst in your mouth. This salad is equally refreshing eaten on its own or as an accompaniment to grilled fish or poultry.

The assortment of colors makes for a spectacular presentation for any occasion. Apparently, in South Africa this salad is served with balsamic vinegar, but the citrus recipe in this book (Bree's Citrus Vinaigrette, page 59) can also be used. Try them both and let your palette make the choice!

Wilderness Mango Salad
Serves 4

1 head *Bibb*, *red leaf*, or *green leaf lettuce*, washed and patted dry
1 medium mango, peeled, pit removed, and cut into 1-inch dice
1 medium English cucumber, cut into 1-inch dice
1/2 small red onion, thinly sliced
8 ounces *feta cheese*, cut into 1-inch dice
1 cup roughly chopped fresh mint leaves
2 tablespoons roughly chopped cilantro, (optional)
2 tablespoons vinaigrette

Arrange lettuce leaves on a colorful serving bowl. Top with mango, cucumber, onion, cheese, mint, and cilantro, if using. Drizzle your choice of vinaigrette over salad.

Elephants in South Africa

Living in the Middle East, tabouleh was served often and in many varieties. It seems that every person had a unique way of making it, but it was always included in a *mezze*—an assortment of hors d'oeuvres or miniature versions of main dishes—in Middle Eastern and Mediterranean restaurants and homes. The number of dishes served in a mezze is optional, but as many as forty would not be uncommon. Mezzes usually precede meals, but if there are enough dishes, it is a meal in itself.

Tabouleh is great as a vegetarian meal, served with hummus and whole wheat pita, or with grilled fish or chicken.

A nice presentation is to arrange romaine lettuce leaves in a serving bowl, spoon tabouleh on top, and garnish with fresh mint leaves. For a richer meal, cooked garbanzo beans can be added. And for a gluten-free version, use the garbanzo beans instead of the bulgur wheat.

In this recipe, I like to use English cucumbers or the tiny and very crunchy ones found in Middle Eastern markets or select grocery stores. Both varieties are relatively seedless, so they are less bitter and much easier to digest. Also, the skins do not need to be peeled. Unfortunately, once you taste either of these varieties, you won't want to go back to the standard types found at your local farms and grocery stores. So my suggestion is to ask your farmer to grow them or grow your own!

The Lebanese way to make tabouleh is a no-cook method. This is great for people on a raw-foods diet, of which there are more and more. The wheat pulls in all the juices from the vegetables and makes for a much tastier version. It is also a lot easier to assemble.

Middle Eastern Tabouleh
Serves 4-6

2/3 cup fine or medium bulgur wheat
1 1/2 bunches flat-leaf parsley, finely chopped
1 large bunch fresh mint, finely chopped
1 cup roughly chopped scallions, green parts included
2 large *tomatoes*, cut into 1/2-inch dice
1 large English cucumber or 4 Lebanese cucumbers, cut into 1/2-inch dice
Juice of 2 lemons, plus extra if needed
1/4 cup extra virgin olive oil, plus extra if needed
Sea salt
Freshly ground black pepper

In a large glass bowl, mix ingredients well; let sit until the wheat has plumped out—approximately 2 hours. Add more lemon juice and olive oil if too dry. Adjust seasoning to taste; refrigerate until ready to use. The tabouleh will keep for up to 3 days in the refrigerator and actually gets better with age—just like you!

Me, in Marrakech, Morocco

This typical Middle Eastern salad is also called a bread salad. You will rarely be served a *mezze* without the incorporation of this refreshing and light dish. Lemon juice and olive oil together are outstanding, but the inclusion of sumac in this recipe adds a nice, fruity-tart flavor. Before lemons were available, the Romans used sumac, so if you do not have this condiment, add a tad more lemon juice. But this is a fun way to experiment with a new flavor you may not already be familiar with. I love to serve this with Lebanese Chicken Za'atar (page 144) or grilled fish and always include this in my Middle Eastern dinners. Sumac can be found in all Middle Eastern markets.

Fatima's Fatoush Salad
Serves 4

3 tomatoes (approximately 1 pound), cut into 1/2-inch dice
1 large English cucumber or 4 Lebanese cucumbers, cut into 1/2-inch dice
1 medium onion, minced
2 cloves garlic, minced
1 romaine lettuce heart, shredded

Salad dressing
2 tablespoons fresh lemon juice
2 tablespoons olive oil
2 tablespoons finely chopped fresh mint
1 teaspoon sumac (optional)
Sea salt
Freshly ground black pepper

4 slices whole wheat pita bread, toasted

In a large bowl, toss tomatoes, cucumbers, onions, garlic, and lettuce. In a small, separate bowl, whisk together lemon juice, olive oil, mint, sumac, sea salt, and pepper. Pour over salad and toss. Just before serving, tear toasted pita bread into bite-size pieces and incorporate into salad.

I have visited Greece on numerous occasions and tasted so many versions of this famous salad, I cannot tell you. The one I prefer was eaten on the beautiful island of Rhodes, situated on the Aegean Sea. I fondly remember sitting in an outdoor taverna with family and friends one glorious summer day. The owner, like most Greek people, treats young children as kings and queens. She totally spoiled my young daughters and treated them to honey–laden baklava following lunch. This salad is quite different from the Greek salads served in North American restaurants—parsley plays an equal role with the lettuce. It is absolutely delicious, and I think you will agree! This dish is sensational as a meal or as an accompaniment to freshly grilled fish. Serve with a rustic whole wheat bread to soak up the dressing.

Rhodes Island Greek Salad
Serves 4

1 small red onion, thinly sliced
1/4 cup Zola's Greek Dressing (page 71)
1 small head *romaine* or *green leaf lettuce*, chopped
2 large bunches flat-leaf parsley, roughly chopped
2 large *tomatoes*, cut into 1/2-inch dice
1/2 English cucumber, sliced
1/2 *green* or *red pepper*, sliced
8 ounces crumbled *feta cheese*
12 Kalamata olives, pits removed

In a small bowl, marinate the onions in the dressing for 15 minutes to render them sweeter. Mix the prepared lettuce leaves and parsley in a medium salad bowl. Top with remaining ingredients, adding onions and dressing. Mix well.

I think my girls order Caesar salad every time we go to a restaurant! My version is a bit different in that I add sliced avocado and homemade croutons for a more flavorful experience. Making one's own croutons is a cinch. Preheat oven to 350°. Use the heels of leftover whole wheat bread, and cut them into small cubes. Place them on a baking sheet and bake in oven for 10 minutes. I think you will enjoy this.

Caesar Salad
Serves 4

1 large head romaine lettuce leaves, torn into bite-size pieces
1 large Haas avocado, peeled, pit removed, sliced lengthwise
1 cup homemade whole wheat croutons or toasted pita chips
1 1/2 cups shaved Parmesan cheese
2 anchovy filets for garnish (optional)
1/2 cup Juliette Caesar's Salad Dressing (page 64)

Place romaine lettuce in a wooden salad bowl. Top with avocado, croutons, Parmesan, and anchovy filets, if using. Toss with salad dressing just before serving.

Variation: Top with grilled shrimp, chicken, or salmon for a main course.

Salads in the Raw and Not So Raw

The first time I visited Morocco, I truly thought I was in the film *1001 Nights*. It seemed so exotic to me at age twenty-two. I remember to this day how the earth smelled—rich and musky. I fell in love with the people, the culture, and the food. No matter how poor the people were, they always invited us to share their famous sweetened mint tea with them. I quickly learned the art of bargaining for anything I purchased, as this is the true way of life in this country. In fact, they would be insulted if you did not take the time to drink tea and bargain.

I tasted cumin, coriander, pepper, mint, paprika, and cinnamon as if it were for the very first time, because these are all harvested there. Until you have tasted *fresh* spices and herbs, you cannot begin to fathom the difference in taste to store-bought brands. Wow! They exude flavor.

Moroccans use these locally grown spices and herbs in their cuisine to make for some incredible concoctions. Of all the countries I have visited, this is one of my favorite cuisines. I love the muskiness of cumin added to soups or the exotic flavor of cinnamon mixed with rice.

The following salad is simple to make and very refreshing served as a side dish. Children love it. The average Moroccan woman is a fabulous cook, having learned from her elders at a young age. Meals are a very important part of life in this country. The average family will not have many gadgets at home, either, and their kitchens will not be modern. There is rarely a food processor, but a grater will be used to prepare the carrots in this dish. So if you do not own a food processor, get out your grater!

Moroccan Carrot Salad
Serves 4

1 pound carrots, grated
1/4 cup beet sugar
1/2 teaspoon cinnamon
1/2 teaspoon ground cumin
1/2 teaspoon ground coriander
1/4 teaspoon sea salt
1/3 cup lemon juice
1/4 cup chopped flat-leaf parsley

Place carrots in a medium bowl. Add the beet sugar, spices and salt. Chill for several hours or overnight so the carrots have time to pull in the flavors of the spices. Just before serving, mix in the lemon juice and chopped parsley.

This salad comes from the south of France, where the wonderful Nicoise olives are found. They are very small and probably one of the most exquisite of all olives, with a rich, nutty flavor. This is a meal in itself and full of flavor and color!

Life in the south of France is almost idyllic. The hustle and bustle of larger European cities is left behind. The climate is almost too good to be true, which makes for a laid-back atmosphere.

One of my jobs while living in Switzerland was working in television for Formula One race car driving. Yes, it was extremely exciting, and one of the highlights was attending the huge television festival in Cannes called MIPTV. How many times have I sat at an outdoor cafe after a long day's work in this magical region, watching the world go by as I sipped my coffee and ate a wonderful meal! The food in this area is of the utmost quality, and you will find this salad in almost any restaurant there.

Living by the ocean and with easy, year-round access to fresh tuna, I prefer to use just that. However, in most recipes, the canned variety is used. In mine, I have also replaced new potatoes with sweet potatoes—the color it adds is like eye candy. Feel free to experiment and use whatever suits your budget. Bon appetit!

An arrangement of Nicoise and assorted olives

Salade Nicoise
Serves 4

2 medium-size sweet *potatoes*, peeled and cut into 1-inch dice
1/2 pound green beans, stems removed
1-pound tuna steak
1 small head *romaine* or *green leaf lettuce*, torn into bite-size pieces
4 hard-boiled *eggs*, peeled and quartered
3-4 *vine-ripened Roma tomatoes*, quartered
1/2 English cucumber, diced
1 sweet *red pepper*, cut into 1/4-inch slices
1 red onion, cut into 1/4-inch slices
20 Nicoise, Moroccan, or black olives, pits removed
4 anchovy fillets for garnish (optional)
6 whole basil leaves for garnish
1/4 cup Mediterranean Anchovy Vinaigrette (page 70) or Bree's Citrus Vinaigrette (page 59)

Steam potatoes in a medium pot until tender, about 10 to 15 minutes; drain and set aside. Place the green beans in a separate pot and steam in unbleached parchment paper until tender crisp, about 4 minutes. Drain beans and put in an ice bath to shock them; drain again. You can make these ahead and refrigerate, if you like.

Meanwhile, sear tuna on a grill or in a sauté pan. Cook to desired doneness. Let rest for several minutes; slice into thin pieces.

Arrange lettuce on a platter. Place eggs on the outer rim of lettuce. Going in a circular motion, add tomatoes, then the cucumber, peppers, and red onion. Top with sweet potatoes, green beans, tuna, and olives. Garnish with anchovy fillets, if using, and basil leaves. Drizzle vinaigrette dressing over salad just before serving.

Salads in the Raw and Not So Raw

Chicken salad can sometimes be rather dreary and boring, but not this one—toasted walnuts are added for crunch, dried cranberries for color and zest, and fresh cilantro for its fragrant mix of parsley and citrus flavors and extra color. If you do not care for cilantro, use flat-leaf parsley instead. By toasting the walnuts, the essential oils are released and the flavor is enhanced. Serve your Celestial Chicken Salad atop a bed of lettuce on a summer evening, as a tea sandwich for light fare, or for heartier fare, as a sandwich filling on whole grain bread. This is also a superb way to use leftover chicken. No one will complain when this delicious chicken salad is seen on the buffet.

Celestial Chicken Salad
Serves 4

1 pound deboned and skinless chicken breasts, cooked, cut into bite-size cubes
1 cup diced celery
1/2 cup dried cranberries
1/2 cup walnuts, toasted
3 tablespoons heavy mayonnaise
2 tablespoons sour cream or Greek-style yogurt
2 tablespoons finely chopped fresh cilantro (optional)
Sea salt
Freshly ground black pepper
Fresh cilantro sprigs for garnish

Place first four ingredients in a medium mixing bowl. Stir in mayonnaise, sour cream, and chopped cilantro, if using; mix well. Season to taste with salt and pepper. Garnish with sprigs of fresh cilantro.

Grapes from my sister and brother-in-law's orchards

Okay, I must admit I have never met anyone who does not like my version of tuna salad. It is sweet and savory at the same time. When you look at the ingredients, don't turn your nose up. It is absolutely delicious! The sunflower seeds give a lovely savory taste, and the raisins complement this with a natural sweetness. Add the chopped celery for crunch, and don't be surprised when people beg you to make this for them! Kids absolutely adore this tuna salad, and it also makes a great sandwich filling.

For me, the key to making this a great-tasting salad is to really mix the tuna and mayonnaise well before you add the other ingredients. It should be a silky texture, but feel free to have a chunkier one if desired.

Lou Lou's Lunar Tunar Salad
Serves 4

2 (8 ounce) cans white albacore tuna, in water, drained
1/2 cup unsulphured raisins
1/2 cup salted sunflower seeds
1/2 cup chopped organic celery
4 tablespoons mayonnaise
Freshly ground black pepper
1 small head of *Bibb* or *red leaf lettuce*, well rinsed
Organic nasturtiums for garnish (optional)

As tuna is naturally salty, there is no need to add any extra salt. Mix all the ingredients together in a medium mixing bowl. Place a lettuce leaf on individual serving plates. Top with tuna salad. Garnish with organic nasturtiums, if desired. They will add beautiful color to your serving plates.

Vegetarians are always looking for ways to incorporate protein into their diet, and this does the trick with the peanut butter. Soba noodles are made with buckwheat flour, which is much healthier than the normal variety. I love anything with peanut butter, and this sauce is really yummy. You can make it as spicy as you like. If you are making a spicier version, sliced cucumbers are great for taking the fire out of your mouth! Typically, sesame noodles are served chilled.

Sesame Noodle Salad
Serves 4

12 ounces soba or buckwheat noodles
4 cups water

Peanut Sauce
2 tablespoons crunchy or creamy peanut butter
2 tablespoons water
2 garlic cloves, crushed
3 scallions, finely chopped
1 tablespoon low-sodium soy sauce
1 tablespoon red wine vinegar
2 tablespoons sunflower oil
1 tablespoon chili sauce
2 tablespoons finely chopped fresh cilantro
2 tablespoons toasted cashew nuts for garnish

Bring water to a boil and add soba noodles. Simmer over low heat for approximately 4 minutes, until tender. Drain well; cool.

Meanwhile, to make the peanut sauce, place all ingredients but cashew nuts in a small saucepan over medium-low heat. Stir constantly until well blended.

Place cooked soba noodles in a large, glass bowl and top with sauce. Place in refrigerator for one hour, or until chilled. Garnish with cashew nuts.

Cayce highly recommended including gelatin in our diets for its ability to increase our vitamin intake from the foods we eat. In one of his readings, the information given was that gelatin in itself is not full of vitamins; however, when it is combined with foods containing specific vitamins, the body is able to extract these, which would not otherwise be possible without the gelatin. (849-75) Cayce recommended using grated carrots, celery, and other vegetables with gelatin as much as three times per week, and to be sure to include their juices in the salad.

When I was growing up as a baby boomer, gelatin salads were eaten in most American and Canadian family homes. Try to return to the old ways of doing things, and start to reintroduce wonderfully invigorating and healthy salads such as this one. I think most people would be pleased to see a gelatin salad at a party or at the dinner table, so I invite you to adapt these old-time recipes to your diet. They are refreshing and great for you!

Lime Gelatin with Grated Vegetables
Serves 4

1 package lime jello
1 cup boiling water
1 cup cold water
1 cup finely chopped *watercress*
1/2 cup grated *celery*
1/2 cup grated carrots

In a medium bowl, pour one cup boiling water over jello. Stir to dissolve; allow to sit for two minutes. Pour one cup of cold water into mixture and stir. Once gelatin has started to gel, mix in raw veggies. Cover tightly with plastic wrap and refrigerate until set.

Salads in the Raw and Not So Raw

Cayce spoke often of the importance of incorporating fresh fruits in one's diet. In fact, he suggested making a meal of fresh fruit occasionally, instead of the usual green salad for lunch. He also mentioned the importance of eating gelatin salads made with fruits, particularly peaches, pears, and pineapple. Be creative in the fruits you use, and enjoy different combinations with gelatin.

This recipe will be popular with the taste buds, but it is also full of nutrients. Now medical research has shown that berries are great for your heart, brain, and total well-being. The pineapple juice is sufficiently sweet to balance any tartness from the fresh berries. Farmers markets are great places to find fresh berries, if you do not grow your own. Always look for brightly colored ones with no mold. Berries need to be rinsed well just before using—they can become soggy and moldy if you wash them and then put them in the refrigerator.

Very Berry Lime Gelatin Salad
Serves 4

1 package lime jello
1 cup boiling water
1 cup pineapple juice
1 cup mixed berries, such as *raspberries*, blueberries, blackberries, or *strawberries*

In a medium bowl, pour one cup boiling water over jello. Stir to dissolve; allow to sit for two minutes. Pour pineapple juice into mixture and stir. Once gelatin has started to gel, mix in berries. Cover tightly with plastic wrap and refrigerate until set.

Some people will make a face and run for the hills when you tell them they are eating raw beets. However, this is a very healthy way to eat this richly hued vegetable and it is actually quite delicious. Add the natural sweetness of oranges to complement and counterbalance the red wine vinaigrette, and you have a salad full of flavor. Another variation on this would be to replace the oranges with Anjou pears, which are a great source of vitamin C.

Toasting the walnuts removes any bitter taste and enhances flavor.

Raw Beet and Orange Salad
Serves 4

3 small beets, scrubbed, peeled, and grated
2 oranges, peeled and sectioned, or 2 Anjou *pears*, diced
1/2 cup walnuts, toasted
4 tablespoons red wine vinaigrette
1 cup finely chopped parsley

In a medium bowl, toss the beets, oranges (or pears), and walnuts with the vinaigrette. Refrigerate for at least an hour. Top beet mixture with chopped parsley just before serving.

Fennel has an almost anise, or licorice, flavor to it and is eaten raw in this salad. The beets have been roasted to give an extra sweetness. Pine nuts are really seeds that have been extracted from pine cones. They are not cheap, but you do not need a lot of them to add depth to your dish. Be sure to purchase quality pine nuts (those imported from China would not be recommended) in an airtight container, as they spoil easily. Toasting pine nuts will bring out their natural, buttery sweetness.

The dressing for this salad is quite natural, with the juice from the oranges added to olive oil, which makes for a very healthy meal. The beets can be roasted a day before making this salad, if desired.

To toast the pine nuts, place them in an ovenproof dish. Use low heat (300°) and bake until they turn a caramel color. If you overcook, they will have a bitter taste.

Shaved Fennel and Beet Salad
Serves 4

2 medium-size beets (approximately 1/2 pound)
3 tablespoons olive oil, divided
2 medium-size fennel bulbs (approximately 1/2 pound), outer core removed, sliced paper thin
2 oranges (approximately 1 pound), peeled and sectioned, juices reserved
1 teaspoon orange zest
1/2 cup toasted pine nuts
Sea salt
Freshly ground black pepper

Preheat oven to 450°. Remove the beet greens and refrigerate for another use. Scrub the beets well with a vegetable brush. Place beets on aluminum foil in an ovenproof dish. Rub with 1 teaspoon olive oil and wrap tightly with foil. Roast in the oven for approximately one hour, or until tender. Once cool enough to handle, peel the beets and slice into 1/4-inch pieces.

To serve, arrange beets, fennel, orange slices, and orange zest in a medium-size salad bowl or on individual salad plates. Sprinkle pine nuts over the salad. Drizzle with remaining olive oil and reserved orange juice; season to taste with salt and pepper.

I always encouraged my girls to cook with me and to be creative in the kitchen. When Bree was 15 years old, she decided overnight to stop eating meat and poultry, after watching a TV special with the famous French actress and animal rights activist Brigitte Bardot. Since that time, she is always inventing new dishes with fish in them, as she loves that source of protein.

One summer while Bree was visiting from Geneva, she created this yummy salad. We love going to the local farmers market to buy fresh corn and whatever is seasonal. Using her words, this is one of the easiest recipes, but so good and tasty, it's worth a lot more! This salad takes minutes to prepare but can be made one day in advance without garnishes and dressing. It is perfect at midday or for a light dinner in the summertime.

Bree's Virginia Beach Summer Salad
Serves 4

1 *red pepper*, cut into 1/2-inch dice
1 *yellow pepper*, cut into 1/2-inch dice
2 (8 ounce) cans albacore tuna, drained
8 ounces crumbled *feta cheese*
1 cup sweet corn, uncooked if seasonal
4 tablespoons Yodeling Yogurt Vinaigrette (page 65)
1/2 cup sunflower seeds
1/2 cup unsulphured raisins
Edible flowers for garnish (optional)

In a large bowl, mix peppers, tuna, feta cheese, and corn. Add yogurt vinaigrette and stir. Refrigerate until ready to serve. Just before serving, garnish with sunflower seeds, raisins, and edible flowers, if desired.

Asian slaw is such a great variation of the usual coleslaw often served at picnics and gatherings. This is indeed a more exciting version and filled with color. It also has a great crunchy texture.

Napa cabbage can now be found in any grocery store or Asian market. If you cannot find fresh snow peas, substitute steamed garden peas. Toasted soy nuts are easily found in the bulk section of health food stores.

Asian Slaw
Serves 4

3 cups shredded Napa cabbage
1 cup roughly shredded carrots
1 cup julienned snow peas
1 *red bell pepper*, finely julienned
1 cup daikon (Japanese) radish, peeled and julienned
1/3 cup chopped scallions, green parts included
1/4 cup roughly chopped fresh cilantro
5 tablespoons Ah-So Asian Dressing (page 68)
1/4 cup toasted soy nuts
1 lime, sliced
2 tablespoons toasted sesame seeds

Place the cabbage, carrots, snow peas, bell pepper, radish, scallions, and cilantro in a large mixing bowl. Pour the vinaigrette over the vegetables and toss to mix evenly. Cover and refrigerate for one hour. Just before serving, mix again to incorporate all the flavors. Garnish with toasted soy nuts, lime slices, and toasted sesame seeds.

This is a delicious combination that can be made in very little time. If you have leftover chicken, try making this for lunch or dinner. By adding steamed vegetables, you have a complete meal. Curry is always exotic-tasting, to me, but if you do not care for it, use chopped fresh herbs, such as parsley or basil, instead. This salad is also delicious spooned into a whole wheat pita pocket with crunchy lettuce or bean sprouts, which makes for a fabulous snack or meal. Alternatively, try it over a bed of crunchy lettuce and top with bean sprouts for an exquisite luncheon treat.

Curried Couscous and Chicken Salad
Serves 4

2 cups vegetable stock
1 cup dry couscous
2 cups cooked chicken, cut into thin strips
1/2 cup diced, steamed carrots
1/2 cup diced, steamed zucchini
1/2 cup steamed peas
1 teaspoon good quality Indian curry powder

In a medium saucepan, bring vegetable stock to a boil. Add couscous; cover; lower heat and allow to simmer for 5 minutes. Turn off heat and remove pan from burner; let stand until all liquid is absorbed, about 10-15 minutes. Fluff with a fork.

In a medium bowl, mix couscous, chicken, and vegetables; add curry powder and stir. Refrigerate for one hour before serving. This will keep for up to 3 days in the refrigerator.

Variation: Use raw vegetables instead of cooked.

Salads in the Raw and Not So Raw

There is nothing more refreshing than a variety of crisp lettuce leaves and fresh herbs to complement any meal. This salad is named after my youngest granddaughter, Sienna Lilly, who, at eighteen months, already adores any salad given to her. In fact, she has a love affair with good food. Sienna enjoys sitting in her grandparents' vegetable garden in the Lake District of Northern Italy, pulling cherry tomatoes from the vines and stuffing them into her mouth. She has never eaten a hot dog or a fast-food item, and I doubt that she ever will.

Now one thing I would love to know? How did I get two grandchildren with blonde hair and blue eyes, when everyone else has brown hair and brown eyes? One of life's mysteries that will reveal itself to us one day. So this is for my youngest blue-eyed baby.

Sienna's Summer Salad
Serves 4

1 small head of Bibb lettuce
1 small bunch of watercress, stems removed, chopped
1 small bunch of fresh mint, finely chopped
1 small bunch of flat-leaf parsley, finely chopped
1 small bunch of fresh basil, chopped
Edible flowers for garnish (optional)

Wash vegetables and herbs thoroughly. Spin in salad spinner until dry. Place salad ingredients in a large, wooden salad bowl. Drizzle with your favorite vinaigrette and garnish with edible flowers, if desired.

Sienna

Anais

Brooke at a market in Lake Como, Italy

There is a natural sweetness and an energizing quality to fruit. On numerous trips to Southeast Asia, I have been impressed with the region's love for fruit salads. They were skillfully displayed on every buffet table, making them even more enticing. The following ingredients are easily available in grocery stores, and although I do not prescribe eating non-local foods, especially imported ones, this is a once-in-a-while treat. Of course, if you live in a tropical climate, this is an alluring way to use your natural resources.

Exotic Fresh Fruit Salad
Serves 6

1 fresh mango, peeled, pit removed
1 small papaya, peeled, pit removed
1 medium *Asian pear,* cored
3 kiwi fruit, peeled
1 cup fresh pineapple
4 ripened Asian bananas, peeled, sliced diagonally
Juice of 1 lime
6 large dates, pit removed, sliced

Dice mango, papaya, Asian pear, kiwi, and pineapple into equal sizes; reserve any juices. Mix fruits and their juices together in a large bowl. Just before serving, slice bananas and squeeze fresh lime juice over them to prevent discoloration. Add bananas and lime juice to mixed fruit. To serve, create a masterful effect by using a clear, glass bowl to present this dessert.

Vinaigrettes and Dressings

There are several ways to make vinaigrettes and dressings. If you are making large quantities for a party or want to have some on hand for a week, my suggestion is to prepare the dressing in a blender. This way, the dressing can be poured into a glass jar and easily stored in the refrigerator until needed.

Another way, which is most common in European homes, is to whisk together all of the dressing ingredients in the bottom of a salad bowl. Then you simply place the desired lettuce and salad ingredients on top and bring the bowl to the table. Just before serving, the salad is tossed and there is no extra mess to clean up.

In most of the following recipes, I have chosen to use a small bowl to incorporate ingredients, but choose the method that works best for you. However you wish to make dressings, I guarantee that no prepackaged or bottled variety can substitute for the simple, preservative-free ones you can make at home with the finest oils and ingredients.

In this section, I advise adjusting seasoning to one's own taste, referring to the addition of sea salt and freshly ground black pepper. By becoming familiar with herbs and spices, you may find that there is less need for salt. Most of us and those we prepare meals for can benefit from reducing sodium in our diet, which is a more healthy choice long term. And I bet you will have fun introducing new tastes to your family and friends by doing so.

Balsamic Vinaigrette
Bree's Citrus Vinaigrette
Anais's Red Wine Vinaigrette
Roberta's Raspberry Vinaigrette
Really Roasted Red Pepper Vinaigrette
Totally Tomato Vinaigrette
Juliette Caesar's Dressing
Yodeling Yogurt Vinaigrette
Fifi's French Dressing
Lola's Lemon Tahini Dressing
Ah-So Asian Dressing
Wonderful Watercress Vinaigrette
Mediterranean Anchovy Vinaigrette
Zola's Greek Dressing
Beautiful Blue Cheese Dressing
Ranch Dressing
Mayonnaise

What makes great balsamic vinaigrette? Just like wine, the quality you purchase! It is up to you and your budget. True balsamic vinegar is made from a reduction of syrup from sweet wine grapes, giving a rich, deep brown color that has both a sweet and a sour taste. And, just like wine, there are hundreds of qualities aged in various types of wooden kegs. This is a great way to top off any fresh salad, and it is so divine, no toppings are needed!

Balsamic Vinaigrette
1 tablespoon balsamic vinegar
1 tablespoon beet sugar
1 tablespoon minced garlic
3 tablespoons extra virgin olive oil
Sea salt
Freshly ground black pepper

Whisk together balsamic vinegar, sugar, and garlic in a small bowl. Add olive oil in drops, and continue whisking until well blended. Adjust seasoning to taste. Store in a glass jar in the refrigerator for up to one week.

Add any of the following for a great variation:
Grain mustard, minced shallot, honey, fresh basil, or any herb you love. I use Herbes de Provence frequently.

Vinaigrettes and Dressings

This is one of my favorite dressings, and I use it frequently in my household. It is also an ideal marinade for fish or chicken. I highly recommend using freshly squeezed (rather than bottled) lemon juice in the recipe when possible. By adding your favorite herbs, you can vary this recipe to your liking. Fresh grapefruit juice or orange juice instead of the lemon juice is also a nice change.

Bree's Citrus Vinaigrette
1 tablespoon freshly squeezed lemon juice
1 teaspoon chopped fresh thyme
3 tablespoons extra virgin olive oil
Sea salt
Cracked black pepper

Whisk ingredients together in a small bowl or glass jar; adjust seasonings to your taste. Store in a glass jar in the refrigerator for up to one week.

Add any of the following for a great variation: Dijon mustard, minced garlic, minced shallot, honey, fresh basil, or any herb you love. I also use Herbes de Provence.

Red wine vinegar has a naturally zesty flavor, which makes for invigorating vinaigrettes. This dressing is wonderful on any field-of-greens salad or with chopped, raw vegetables.

Anais's Red Wine Vinaigrette
1 tablespoon Dijon-style mustard
1 tablespoon red wine vinegar
3 tablespoons grape seed oil
1 teaspoon Herbes de Provence
Sea salt
Cracked black pepper

Whisk ingredients together in a small bowl; adjust seasoning to your taste. Store in a glass jar in the refrigerator for up to one week.

Vinaigrettes and Dressings

This is a more mellow version of this modern-day dressing, and if you have homemade jam or can buy it locally made at your farmer's market, all the better! Actually, you can use any flavor of jam to create your own vinaigrette—strawberry, blueberry, peach, fig, and on and on.

Roberta's Raspberry Vinaigrette
1 tablespoon *raspberry jam*
1 tablespoon red wine vinegar
3 tablespoons extra virgin olive oil
Sea salt
Cracked black pepper

Whisk ingredients together in a small bowl or glass jar; adjust seasoning to your taste. Refrigerate in a glass jar for up to one week.

This dressing was a totally unexpected discovery. I was making sauce for my turkey loaf and had a bit left over. By adding olive oil and seasonings, this absolutely delicious dressing was created. It has countless uses, but it is particularly tasty over a hearty lettuce, such as romaine or Belgian endive.

A jar of roasted red peppers may be used instead of freshly roasted, of course, but it will not be quite as much fun or give you the same sense of authenticity. Why not give it a try!

Really Roasted Red Pepper Vinaigrette
1 r*ed bell pepper*, roasted, skinned, and seeded
    or 6- to 8-ounce jar *roasted red peppers*, drained
10 *sun-dried tomatoes*, drained of excess oil, diced
1 clove garlic, crushed
1 small shallot, diced
1/4 cup extra virgin olive oil
1 tablespoon fresh thyme or 1 teaspoon dried
Sea salt
Cracked black pepper

To roast the pepper, grill over an open flame or broil on a baking sheet in the oven, turning until charred on all sides. Remove from heat and place in a paper bag until cool enough to peel off skin; peel pepper and discard seeds.

Place ingredients in a blender and mix until velvety smooth. Adjust seasoning to your taste. Refrigerate in a glass jar for up to 3 days.

Vinaigrettes and Dressings

This is another versatile and unusual dressing that is fabulous in summer or winter months. It is also a refreshing sauce served on grilled sea bass, halibut, rockfish, or other white fish. Or drizzle the dressing on top of an all-green salad, top it with cottage cheese and a black olive, and you have an eye-pleasing and colorful plate.

When locally grown tomatoes are unavailable, use organic tomato paste instead.

Totally Tomato Vinaigrette
1 large *vine-ripened tomato,* seeded
　or 2 tablespoons *tomato paste*
2 cloves garlic, minced
1/2 small red onion, chopped
4 large fresh basil leaves, roughly chopped
1/2 cup extra virgin olive oil
1/4 cup red wine vinegar
Sea salt
Cracked black pepper

Place all ingredients in a blender and mix until velvety smooth. Adjust seasoning to your taste. Store in a glass jar in refrigerator for up to one week.

When I was a young girl, my mother used to take me to a superb restaurant called Café Martin on Mountain Street in Montreal. That is where I learned to love Caesar salad. Impeccably dressed waiters would arrive at our table to prepare the exquisite dressing in huge wooden salad bowls. This is not the original Caesar dressing that I tasted there, which is made with raw eggs and fresh anchovies, but I think you will love the simplicity of making this one as well as the creamy consistency.

Juliette Caesar's Dressing
2 cloves garlic, finely minced
1 tablespoon anchovy paste (optional)
1/4 cup grated Parmesan cheese
1/4 cup mayonnaise
1/4 cup freshly squeezed lemon juice
1 teaspoon Worcestershire sauce
Sea Salt
Cracked black pepper

Whisk ingredients together in a small bowl; adjust seasoning to your taste. Store in a glass jar in the refrigerator for up to one week.

Swiss homes and restaurants will typically serve this creamy vinaigrette with Bibb lettuce, cucumber slices, and tomato wedges. It is light, refreshing, and versatile. Soy yogurt will easily transform this recipe into a vegan dish. And for a great dressing to go with Indian dishes, substitute a pinch of cumin and curry powder for the fresh herbs.

Yodeling Yogurt Vinaigrette
1 cup *yogurt* or *soy yogurt*
1 tablespoon Dijon mustard
5 tablespoons extra virgin olive oil
1 teaspoon finely chopped chives
1 teaspoon finely chopped parsley
Zest of 1 organic lemon
Sea salt
Cracked black pepper

Whisk ingredients together in a small bowl; adjust seasoning to your taste. Store in a glass jar in the refrigerator for up to one week.

This dressing is another gem, and kids seem to love it. It is especially good served on leafy green or red lettuce. To add another dimension, top with cooked shrimp, tomato wedges, and avocado slices. Be sure to use only organic ketchup.

Fifi's French Dressing
3 tablespoons organic ketchup
3 tablespoons mayonnaise or soy mayonnaise
1 tablespoon freshly squeezed lemon juice
1 teaspoon Worcestershire sauce
Sea salt
Cracked black pepper

Whisk ingredients together in a small bowl; adjust seasoning to your taste. Store in a glass jar in the refrigerator for up to one week.

Tahini is a smooth paste made from ground sesame seeds. It can be found in the international or organic section of grocery or health food stores, and commonly in Middle Eastern markets. Anything with tahini and lemon juice calls to me. This is not only great on salads, it's a great dipping sauce as well. It can also be used as a wonderful sandwich spread. Try it on whole wheat pita bread with romaine lettuce, tomatoes, cucumber, Kalamata olives, and feta cheese—what I call my Greek salad sandwich. Spectacular!

Lola's Lemon Tahini Dressing
4 tablespoons tahini
2 tablespoon freshly squeezed lemon juice
2 tablespoons lemon zest
Black pepper or dash of cayenne pepper

Whisk ingredients together in a small bowl; adjust seasoning to your taste. If dressing becomes too thick, add a bit of water. Store in a glass jar in the refrigerator for up to one week.

This dressing is great with an Asian-inspired meal or as a marinade. The freshly grated ginger gives it a real zing to heighten your senses and thrill your palette.

Ah-So Asian Dressing
3 tablespoons sunflower oil
3 tablespoons orange juice
3 tablespoons red wine vinegar
1 teaspoon sesame oil
1 teaspoon honey
1 teaspoon freshly grated ginger
Cracked black pepper

Whisk ingredients together in a small bowl; adjust seasoning to your taste. Store in a glass jar in the refrigerator for up to one week.

Vinaigrettes and Dressings

One typically associates watercress with England and those delightful tea sandwiches. But here it is transformed into a delicious and incredibly nutritious dressing to go on field greens (spring mix). The naturally light and peppery taste of the watercress pairs beautifully with the rich, nutty flavor of walnut oil, a great source of Omega 3s, as well. Top the greens with toasted walnuts for a gourmet touch.

Wonderful Watercress Vinaigrette
1 head *watercress*, well washed and chopped
1/4 cup walnut oil
5 teaspoons red wine vinegar
Sea Salt
Cracked black pepper
1/4 cup toasted walnuts (optional)

Bring a small pot of lightly salted water to a boil. Add watercress and simmer for 5 minutes; drain well. In a small bowl, measure out 1 cup of drained watercress and add walnut oil and apple cider vinegar; season with salt and black pepper. Mix well by hand until a silky texture, or place all ingredients in a blender and mix for several seconds. Top salad with toasted walnuts, if desired.

Unity Library & Archives
1901 NW Blue Parkway
Unity Village, MO 64065

People may think that they really don't like anchovies... until they taste this savory vinaigrette made with the tiny little fish so typical in the Mediterranean countries. Actually, unless someone is allergic to fish, I would not even tell my guests what this is made of and see how they react. Imagine yourself sitting by the sea in an outdoor restaurant in Portofino, Italy, watching the fishing boats and yachts come in.

Mediterranean Anchovy Vinaigrette
1 teaspoon Dijon mustard
1 clove garlic, crushed
4 anchovy fillets in olive oil, drained and finely chopped
6 tablespoons lemon juice
1/2 cup extra virgin olive oil
1/2 cup sunflower oil
Sea salt
Cracked black pepper

To make the vinaigrette, place the mustard, garlic, and anchovy fillets in a small glass bowl. Mix well. Using a whisk, blend in the lemon juice. Slowly whisk in the olive oil and the sunflower oil until the dressing is creamy. Adjust seasoning to your taste. Store in a glass jar in the refrigerator for up to one week.

Vinaigrettes and Dressings

Oregano is an ingredient in many Greek recipes. Paired with basil, as in this recipe, it makes for a delicious dressing. Use it on the Rhodes Island Greek Salad (page 39). Be sure to have some hearty bread on hand to sop up any dressing left on your plate!

Zola's Greek Dressing
3 teaspoons grain mustard
1 clove garlic, pressed
1/2 teaspoon dried oregano
1/2 teaspoon dried basil
1/3 cup red wine vinegar
1 cup extra virgin olive oil
1/4 teaspoon salt
1/4 teaspoon cracked black pepper

In a small mixing bowl, mix grain mustard, garlic, and herbs until well blended. Add vinegar and mix well. Slowly add olive oil, stirring constantly until you have a thick sauce. Season with salt and pepper. Store in a glass jar in the refrigerator for up to one week.

At a Greek fest in Washington, D.C.

This cheese was introduced to me at a young age, as my mother always included a nice wedge of it on her cheese trays when entertaining. People (excluding blue cheese lovers, of course) often think of blue cheese as being a bit stinky. In truth, it is, if it is served on its own. Mixed with sour cream, buttermilk, or mayonnaise, however, it will become a favorite in most households.

If using this dressing on a salad, I suggest using a hearty green lettuce, such as romaine or Belgian endive—it will be too heavy for a softer lettuce. Try serving this dressing on grilled chicken or grilled asparagus, as well, for a robust and distinctive flavor.

Beautiful Blue Cheese Dressing
1/4 cup *sour cream*
1/3 cup *buttermilk*
1 1/2 cups mayonnaise
1 tablespoon fresh lemon juice
1/2 teaspoon Worcestershire sauce
8 ounces crumbled *blue cheese*

Combine all ingredients except the blue cheese in a medium bowl; whisk until smooth. Add blue cheese and mix gently for a chunky dressing. For a smoother dressing, mix until well blended. For a silky texture, mix all ingredients in a blender. Store in a glass jar in the refrigerator for up to one week.

Vinaigrettes and Dressings

This is the famous dressing American and Canadian children seem to love on salads or served as a dip with chips or raw vegetables. However, this version is surprisingly delicious without any sugar, so why not make your own and throw away the store-bought version! This is truly scrumptious and will easily become a favorite.

Ranch Dressing
2 tablespoons finely chopped flat-leaf parsley
1 shallot, peeled and finely minced
2 cloves garlic, peeled and minced
1 teaspoon lemon zest
1 cup *sour cream*
1 tablespoon grain mustard
1/2 cup *buttermilk*
1/4 cup fresh lemon juice
1 tablespoon Worcestershire sauce
1/2 teaspoon white pepper

In a medium bowl, whisk the ingredients until well blended and smooth. Store in a glass jar in the refrigerator for up to one week.

When I first moved to Geneva, I was amazed at how easily people whipped up homemade mayonnaise. It was like nothing I had ever tasted. At that time, most people made it by hand, but a food processor makes it a lot easier. Steamed artichokes become a delicacy when served with this velvety mixture. In France, *crudités* (a selection of raw vegetables) are served with *aioli* (garlic mayonnaise) to make for a splendid appetizer. Once you try this silky mayonnaise on your salads and sandwiches, it will be difficult to imagine using store-bought brands any longer. Homemade mayo is also much healthier. Be sure to use organic eggs.

Mayonnaise
Makes 1 cup

1 or 2 garlic cloves, crushed
1 heaping tablespoon Dijon mustard
2 egg yolks, room temperature
1 cup extra virgin olive oil
4 tablespoons lemon juice
Sea salt
Freshly ground black pepper

Place the garlic, mustard, and egg yolks in the bowl of your food processor; mix well. With motor running, add olive oil by drops until the mixture begins to thicken. Then add the oil in a thin stream until the mixture becomes thick. Thin the sauce with the lemon juice, and season to taste with salt and pepper. Store in a small glass container for up to 2 days.

Variation: Add chopped fresh parsley and drained anchovy fillets.

Warm Your Soul Soups

Growing up in Eastern Canada, soup was considered a staple food in most family homes. To say our winters were long and chilly is an understatement! I used to love coming home after a long day at school, trudging through the snow to the smell of onions, garlic, and celery simmering in our kitchen. The rest of the pot would be filled gradually to make a great meal. Some of the recipes included in this section are soups I gladly ate as a child and continue to feed to my delighted family and loved ones to this day.

I hope you will throw away your cans and bring out your pots once you try your hand at making homemade soups! I guarantee you, nobody will run away at mealtime, and you may find some "extras" showing up at your doorstep as the aromas waft through the neighborhood.

Soups are an excellent way to use extra vegetables and fruits. Homemade vegetable, beef, chicken, and fish stocks are relatively easy to make. A great technique for freezing them is to pour the stock into ice cube trays, and once frozen, transfer the cubes to ziplock bags. That way, you never have to buy store brands, which often contain an excess of sodium, are expensive, and never quite have that optimum taste of homemade. I believe stocks are one of the key ingredients to great soup-making.

I never put flour in my soups! Instead, for most of my soups I prepare what is known in French as a *mirepoix*, a mixture of chopped onions, garlic, celery, and carrots, which I sauté in olive oil to slowly bring out the flavors. This is the base to most soups in this chapter; it is also why my soups are full of flavor. Many people tell me that their homemade soups never taste great and want to know how they can thicken them without using flour. This is the answer.

Soups do take a bit of time to cook. And for the most part, the longer they cook, the tastier they will be. If you're a person on the go, using a slow cooker is a great way to have a meal ready for your return from work at the end of a long day. Sometimes, if I have a bit of soup left over, I will use it as a base for a new concoction. Once you become adept at soup-making, you will see how many uses your creations will have!

In the summer months, there is a wide range of soups that can be served chilled, and the use of locally grown vegetables and fruits will particularly heighten the taste. Kids usually get a kick out of a chilled melon soup served in a hollowed-out cantaloupe shell. Chilled cucumber soup is one of my all-time favorites to start off an elegant dinner party in the warm evenings of summer. It is so easy to make, but so very full of flavor—the fresh herbs from your garden or market make all the difference.

As anyone with a vegetable garden can attest, zucchini grows like weeds. As fall approaches, friends may arrive at your doorstep laden with the fruits of their labor—most likely, zucchini. One of the easiest soups to make in this chapter is a classic French cream of zucchini. It is by far one of the creamiest and most delightful ways to use this great vegetable. There are so few ingredients, and it can be made in twenty minutes flat.

While staying near Versailles with French friends for a recent birthday, I watched in awe at how simply my friend Marina put together this soup. I thank her to this day when people tell me it is the best soup they have ever eaten.

Equally as simple to make is gazpacho, using vine-ripened tomatoes kissed by the summer sun. Rich and inexpensive yet exquisite by the addition of a variety of fresh herbs, who wouldn't like this variety of homemade soup?

As always, I encourage people to be creative in the kitchen and to have fun. Soups are an excellent way to show off your artistic talents and serve healthy meals at the same time. Topping soups with your own homegrown organic sprouts is an excellent way to add protein and vitamins.

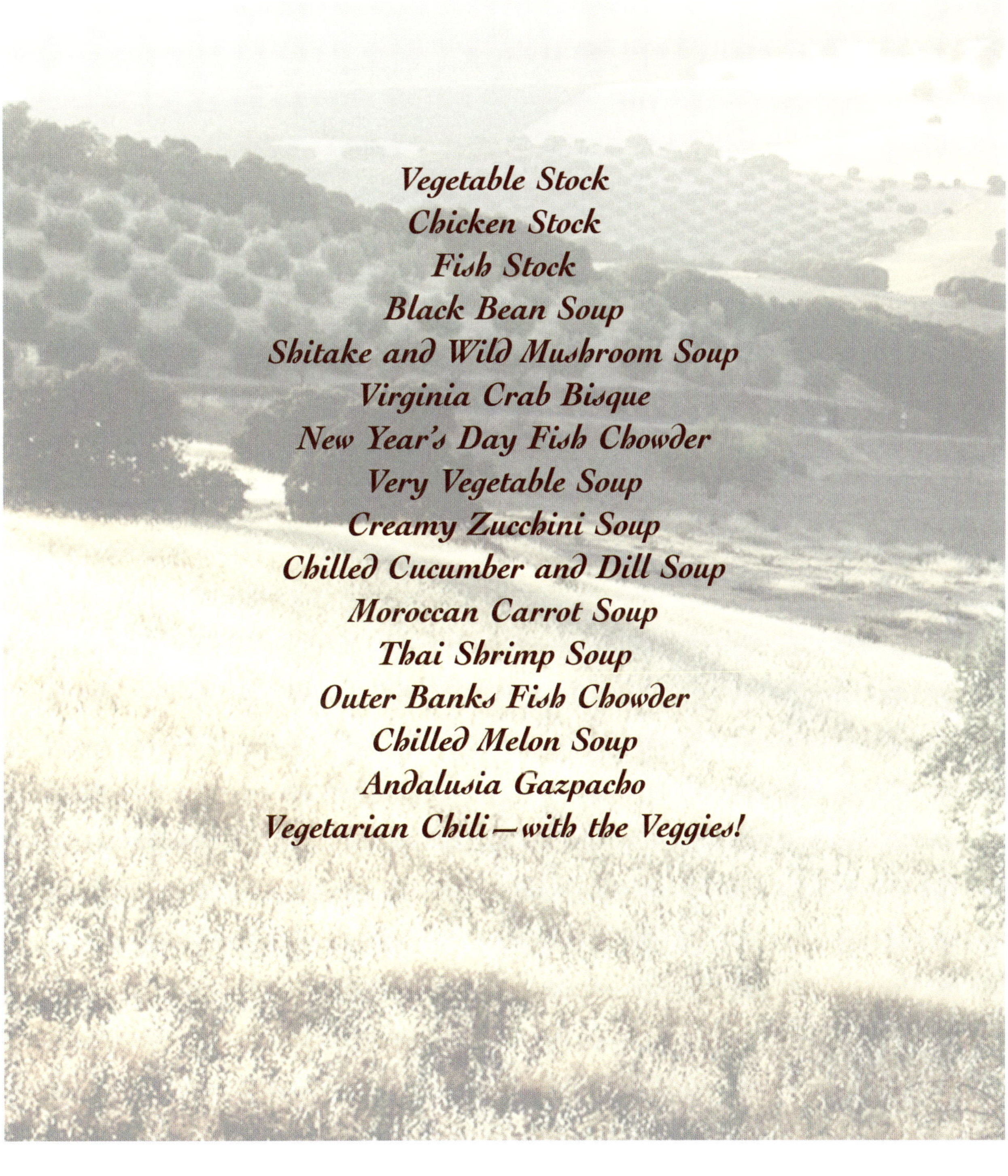

Vegetable Stock
Chicken Stock
Fish Stock
Black Bean Soup
Shitake and Wild Mushroom Soup
Virginia Crab Bisque
New Year's Day Fish Chowder
Very Vegetable Soup
Creamy Zucchini Soup
Chilled Cucumber and Dill Soup
Moroccan Carrot Soup
Thai Shrimp Soup
Outer Banks Fish Chowder
Chilled Melon Soup
Andalusia Gazpacho
Vegetarian Chili—with the Veggies!

Stocks are relatively painless to make, and having them on hand for soups, risottos, or other dinners can make all the difference in the outcome of your endeavors. To be handy for future use, pour the cooled stock into ice cube trays and freeze. Place frozen stock cubes into zip-lock bags, and refreeze until ready to use.

Vegetable Stock
Makes 10 Cups

4 *celery* stalks, chopped
2 large carrots, chopped
1 large onion, including skin, quartered
2 leeks, well washed and roughly chopped
1 parsnip, chopped
1 large *tomato,* chopped
1 *sweet pepper*, chopped
3 sprigs fresh thyme
1 bay leaf
1 bunch parsley, including stems, roughly chopped
1 teaspoon sea salt
1 teaspoon freshly ground black pepper
15 cups water

Put all ingredients into a large stockpot. Bring to a boil and simmer on low heat for 30-40 minutes, stirring occasionally. Take off heat and let cool. Strain over a large bowl, reserving the stock; discard vegetables. Cool stock to room temperature; may be refrigerated for up to one week or frozen for future use.

Warm Your Soul Soups

There is nothing quite like homemade chicken stock. If you can afford it, try making yours with a whole organic chicken. Cooked slowly, this makes for the very best base for chicken soup and any recipe requiring chicken stock.

Chicken Stock
Makes 10 Cups

3-pound whole *chicken* or 3 pounds *chicken* parts, including necks and backs
14 cups water
1 tablespoon olive oil
2 large onions, including skin, quartered
2 large *celery* stalks, chopped
2 large carrots, chopped
Small handful of parsley sprigs, chopped
2-3 sprigs fresh thyme
2 teaspoons sea salt
5 peppercorns

Rinse chicken well and place in a large stockpot; cover with water. Heat to boiling; reduce heat and skim foam from surface; cover and simmer for 1 hour. Add remaining ingredients; cover pot partially and simmer over low heat for 3 to 4 hours. Strain stock and let cool to room temperature; reserve chicken and debone when cooled sufficiently. Refrigerate or freeze chicken for another dish. Refrigerate cooled stock for 1 hour; skim off fat that will have risen to the surface. Refrigerate up to one week or freeze for future use.

Of all the stocks, fish stock is the simplest one to make. Your local fish market or grocery store will gladly put together fish bones, heads, and trimmings of white fish for the asking. Cooked crab shells and lobster shell pieces can also be used instead of the fish to make your stock.

Fish Stock
Makes 5 cups

2 pounds fish bones, heads, and trimmings from white fish
6 cups water
1 onion, chopped
2 *celery* stalks, chopped
1 carrot, chopped
1 bay leaf
2 sprigs fresh parsley
3 black peppercorns
2 teaspoons sea salt
1/2 cup white wine (optional)

Rinse fish bits under cold running water. Add all ingredients to a large stockpot; bring to a boil. Skim foam from the surface. Simmer uncovered for 30 minutes. Strain the stock and discard all bits; cool to room temperature. May be refrigerated for up to 2 days or frozen for up to one month.

Beans, beautiful beans! Black beans have many healthful virtues and add a velvety texture to soups. This hearty soup is best enjoyed in the fall and winter months, with a little ground cumin and coriander to give a smoky taste. I always use dried beans to make this soup, but if you are in a hurry, canned beans will provide the same amount of fiber and protein. Add a dollop of sour cream and serve with whole wheat pita chips.

Black Bean Soup
Serves 8

1 tablespoon olive oil
2 medium onions, chopped
5 garlic cloves, crushed
3 carrots, chopped
3 stalks celery, chopped
4 cups (24 ounces) dried black beans, soaked overnight and drained or 1 (24-ounce) can black beans
10 cups vegetable stock
2 sweet potatoes, cut into large chunks
1 teaspoon ground cumin
1/2 teaspoon ground coriander
Sea salt
White pepper

Heat oil in a large stockpot. Add onions, garlic, carrots, and celery. Cook over medium-high heat for 15 minutes. Add black beans, vegetable stock, sweet potatoes, cumin, and coriander. Cover and cook for about 1 hour, until beans are soft. If you have an immersion blender, puree the bean mixture in the pot for a few seconds until desired consistency. If using a food processor or regular blender, puree one cup of the bean mixture and return it to the pot. Season to taste with salt and pepper.

This soup is heaven for mushroom lovers. It has a definite nutty flavor and is synonymous with autumn, to me, when mushrooms are in season. Dried mushrooms add such depth when cooked and fortunately can be found in almost any grocery store. Of course, if you have access to fresh wild mushrooms, do use these. This soup is nothing like the canned cream of mushroom soup so many people use in their cooking. There is no cream, so it is low in fat, yet I think you'll find that the flavor is far superior to the canned version. Accompanied with toasted, hearty, whole wheat bread, you will have a satisfying meal, whether you are a vegetarian or not.

Shitake and Wild Mushroom Soup
Serves 6

1 tablespoon olive oil
1 large onion, chopped
2 cloves garlic, crushed
2 *celery* stalks, chopped
1 cup dried mixture of wild and shitake mushrooms or 2 cups fresh, chopped
8 cups *chicken* stock or vegetable stock
1 teaspoon Worcestershire sauce
Sea salt
Freshly ground black pepper
Small bunch flat-leaf parsley, including stems, chopped, for garnish

Pour olive oil into a medium pot. Add onions, garlic, and celery, and cook until translucent. Add mushrooms, stock, and Worcestershire sauce. Cover and simmer over medium-high heat for 40 minutes, stirring occasionally. Season to taste with salt and pepper. Garnish with fresh parsley.

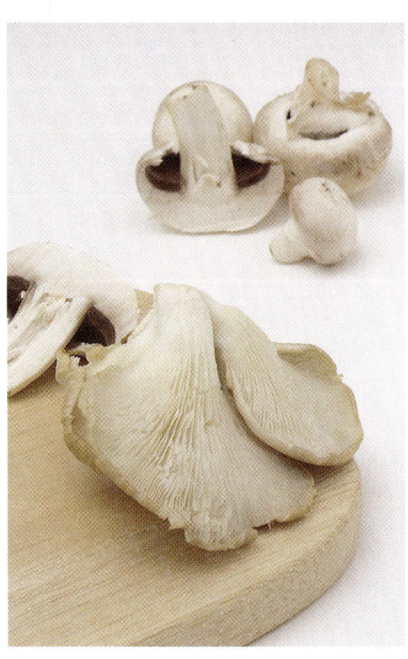

Warm Your Soul Soups

Living in Virginia has its advantages. One of them is the beautiful Chesapeake Bay, which is about 200 miles long, stretching from Havre de Grace, Maryland, to Virginia Beach, Virginia. Blue crabs, as well as soft shell crabs, are often featured on local seafood restaurant menus, and many of the local chefs vie to create the best crab bisque. I prefer using only lump crab meat in mine (wouldn't anyone?) and do not like it to be so full of cream that cream is all you taste, but a combination of back fin or claw meat and lump crab meat is quite tasty and a little easier on the pocketbook. This is a delicious meal served with whole grain bread or crackers.

Virginia Crab Bisque
Serves 6

4 tablespoons unsalted *butter*
1 small onion, chopped
2 *celery* stalks, chopped
5 cups fish stock
1 tablespoon *tomato paste*
1 1/2 pounds lump crab meat or combination back fin, claw, and lump crab meat
3 tablespoons brandy or sherry (optional)
2/3 cup heavy *cream*
3 tablespoons chopped parsley
Sea salt
White pepper
Cayenne pepper (optional)

Melt butter over low heat in a medium pot; add onion and celery and cook until translucent. Add the fish stock, tomato paste, crab meat, and brandy and cook for 10 minutes. Blend in heavy cream and parsley and heat through. Season to taste with salt and pepper.

If you like a bit of spice, add cayenne pepper.

This chowder is adapted from one my mum and grandmother used to make. New Brunswick, Canada, has a huge fishing industry, so you can imagine how many ways we were taught to prepare fish! The Bay of Fundy is one of the coldest waters imaginable, which also makes for the best lobster in the world, or so we like to brag! Scallops, cod, mackerel, and halibut are also outstanding. I actually used to eat leftover lobster for breakfast as a kid.

We also boast some of the best salmon fishing in the world, on the Miramachi River, where United States presidents and many famous personalities have vacationed for the thrill of the catch of this Omega-3-rich fish. At the river lodges, cooks prepare your catch over charcoal grills while you sit outside and enjoy the star-studded skies and falling stars, if you're really lucky.

On New Year's Day in my village, we would be served huge bowls of this fish chowder to help bring in a prosperous and happy beginning. I continue this tradition even though I live in the South. Any leftovers are gladly taken home by one and all! This soup is a meal in itself, and the fresher the fish, the better, but frozen can be substituted.

New Year's Day Fish Chowder
Serves 8

1 cup (2 sticks) *butter*
3 tablespoons olive oil
2 cups diced yellow onions
3 cloves garlic, minced
4 *celery* stalks, diced
2 carrots, peeled and diced
1 large sweet *potato,* diced
1 pound firm, white fish (preferably halibut or cod)
1/2 pound scallops
1/2 pound shrimp, shelled and deveined
1/2 pound lobster or crab meat (canned is fine)
2 quarts organic whole *milk*
1 bay leaf
2 tablespoons Herbes de Provence
Sea salt
Freshly ground black pepper
Cayenne pepper (optional)
4 tablespoons chopped flat-leaf parsley, for garnish

Melt butter in a large pot. Add olive oil, onions, garlic, and celery, and cook until softened but not browned, approximately 10 minutes. Add remaining ingredients except for seasonings and parsley; turn heat to medium on your stove top. Cover and let soup simmer, not boil, for 30 minutes, until all the flavors have married. Add seasonings, and garnish with chopped parsley.

Serve with toasted garlic bread or a hearty Irish soda bread with parsley butter.

Kennebecasis River, New Brunswick, Canada

This soup is just as named—full of fresh vegetables. No matter the time of year, vegetable soup is one of the best for a midday or evening meal and an easy way to incorporate fiber and vitamins into your diet. This recipe is a natural for the summer months when vegetable gardens are overflowing. In the winter months, try to include as many locally grown winter vegetables as possible. One of the keys to making good soups is including plenty of fresh celery.

Very Vegetable Soup
Serves 6

2 tablespoons sunflower oil
2 medium onions, chopped
2 leeks, white part only, sliced and well washed
4 celery stalks, chopped
3 carrots, sliced
2 cloves garlic, crushed
7 cups vegetable stock
2 cups diced yellow squash
1 cup shelled butter beans
1 cup chopped zucchini
3 tomatoes, chopped
1 cup chopped green beans
2 sprigs fresh thyme
Sea salt
Freshly ground black pepper
Fresh herbs for garnish

Heat sunflower oil in a large stockpot. Add onions, leeks, celery, carrots, and garlic, and cook for about 5 minutes, until soft. Add vegetable stock, yellow squash, butter beans, zucchini, tomatoes, green beans, and thyme. Bring to a boil, cover, and cook gently for 20 minutes. Season to taste with salt and pepper. Garnish with fresh herbs.

This soup has a nice, velvety texture, and I have yet to meet anyone who doesn't like the mellow flavors. It can be put on baby's menu early on, and it's also a great way to introduce zucchini to people of all ages. What I particularly love about this soup is the ease and rapidity with which it can be made.

Creamy Zucchini Soup
Serves 4

1 tablespoon sunflower oil
1 medium onion, chopped
2 pounds zucchini, chopped
4 cups vegetable or *chicken* stock
1 tablespoon Herbes de Provence or fresh herbs of your choice
8 ounces *cream cheese*
Sea salt
Freshly ground black pepper

Heat oil in a medium pot. Add onions and cook until translucent. Add zucchini and stock. Cover partially and cook over medium heat for 30 minutes, until zucchini is tender. Puree vegetables in the pot with an immersion blender, or transfer soup to your blender; puree. Stir in herbs and cream cheese until blended. Season to taste with salt and pepper. Voila!

This is a refreshing chilled soup often served in Greece. However, the first time I tried it was at my English friend's home on a warm summer evening. Pauline is definitely British, with such a ducky accent after all these years, and lives in Virginia Beach, where she has recreated the most typical of English cottages you can imagine. Her garden could easily be featured in any house and gardens magazine. Everywhere you go on her property, there is something unique to look at. After these many years of knowing her, I find something new each time.

Pauline used fresh dill from her garden to prepare her soup, which made it all the more spectacular. If you do not like fresh dill, try using fresh spearmint leaves, but never the two together. I like to use English cucumbers in my version of this soup, as they are much easier to digest than some other varieties.

This is a great meal for anyone on a low-fat regimen. However, whether watching your fat intake or not, it is actually very filling and perfect for the summer months.

Chilled Cucumber and Dill Soup
Serves 6

3 medium English cucumbers, peeled and quartered (about 5 cups)
1/2 cup chopped sweet onion (Vidalia or Maui)
1 clove garlic, minced
1/2 cup fresh dill sprigs or fresh spearmint
1 quart nonfat *buttermilk*
1 1/2 cups nonfat plain *yogurt*
Sea salt
Freshly ground black pepper
Pinch of cayenne pepper (optional)
Whole wheat croutons
Edible flowers for garnish
Fresh dill or spearmint for garnish

Combine cucumber, onion, garlic, and dill in a blender and puree until smooth. Blend in buttermilk and yogurt. Season to taste with salt, pepper, and cayenne, if using. Refrigerate for at least 2 to 3 hours before serving.

Ladle into soup bowls. Top with whole wheat croutons and garnish as desired.

Moroccans truly have a wonderful cuisine, and this is a very popular soup in Morocco. I actually first ate this soup at the home of friends, overlooking the Ourika Valley in the Atlas Mountains of Morocco. Do not ask me how they built their "castle," as the roads are made of dirt and they flood when it rains, which happened one day while we visited. They took us to the wonderful Jemmaa Souk, or as the locals call it, the Friday Souk, which is a region mainly inhabited by Berbers. Our host, Az, always has a bag of candies to give to the children when he drives up or down the mountain. I am quite afraid of heights, and the Atlas Mountains have always been a challenge for me—whoever is sitting next to me ends up with a black and blue mark on their arms! Our visit was during Ramadan, and Gertrude, who is also known as "the German Doctor" in Marrakech, made us this delightful soup using locally grown carrots.

Fresh ginger added to the natural sweetness of carrots is quite complementary. Adding the grated fresh nutmeg and ground cinnamon truly creates a taste of Morocco. This soup is pureed, and if you have an immersion blender, that makes it all the easier. If not, use your blender or food processor and puree it in batches.

Moroccan Carrot Soup
Serves 6

1 tablespoon unsalted *butter*
1 onion, chopped
2-inch piece fresh ginger, grated
5 cups peeled and sliced carrots
1 sweet *potato,* chopped
5 cups vegetable stock
Pinch of grated nutmeg
1/4 teaspoon ground cinnamon
1/2 cup orange juice
Sea salt
Freshly ground black pepper
6 edible flowers for garnish

Melt butter in a medium pot. Add onions and ginger and cook for about 5 minutes, until translucent. Add carrots, sweet potatoes, and vegetable stock. Cover and simmer for 30 minutes, until the carrots and potatoes are tender.

Puree soup. Stir in nutmeg, cinnamon, and orange juice. Season to taste with salt and pepper. Ladle into soup bowls and garnish with organic edible flowers, if desired.

Preparing for Ramadan feast

Warm Your Soul Soups

My trips to Southeast Asia have been some of the most exciting of my life. The people are so kind and polite, with a culture that is so different from ours. The hotels are luxurious, with service not to be duplicated anywhere on earth, in my opinion.

The first time I visited Bangkok, at age twenty-four, I stayed at the famous Oriental Hotel on the Chao Phraya River. Bangkok is a vibrant city, both traditional and modern. Not only is it beautiful, it affords a gastronomical experience, as well. It was here that I learned to love lemongrass. I had never tasted Thai food before, although many restaurants now serve this healthy cuisine in America and Canada.

Asian markets are your best bet for finding coconut milk and lemongrass, but most grocery stores now carry these products.

You can create a Thai ambiance by using bamboo place mats.

Thai Shrimp Soup
Serves 4

2 cups *chicken* stock or vegetable stock
2 sticks lemongrass, smashed, tough ends removed, cut into 2-inch pieces
1-inch piece ginger root, peeled and grated
2 tablespoons lime juice
1 cup quartered button mushrooms
4 scallions, chopped
1/2 teaspoon chopped fresh hot chili pepper
16 large shrimp, peeled and deveined
1 (8-ounce) package firm tofu, drained and chopped
3 tablespoons fish sauce
2 cups coconut milk
Fresh cilantro for garnish
4 lime slices for garnish

Heat stock in a medium pot. Add prepared lemongrass, ginger, and lime juice. Cover and boil for 2 minutes. Add mushrooms, scallions, chili pepper, shrimp, tofu, and fish sauce. Cook until shrimp is pink, about 5 minutes. Stir in coconut milk and simmer for 2 minutes. Ladle into soup bowls and garnish with cilantro and slices of lime.

The Outer Banks in North Carolina is one of the most relaxing places to take a break from the hectic pace of reality. My best friend, Jane, built a beautiful home in Corolla. It is situated on a lake yet within minutes of the Atlantic Ocean. Some residents actually have to drive 4-wheel-drive vehicles on the beach to get to their homes, built behind enormous sand dunes. This part of the world is enchanting, and wild horses (Mustangs) can still be seen roaming around at the northernmost tips. And yes, the horses are protected. In fact, it is against the law to go within fifty feet of them. Our good friends Sally and Arlene are on horse patrol to ensure that people respect the laws of the wild.

Locals who live here year-round often spend their time line fishing from the beach, volunteering their time to save the giant turtles, driving the beaches to ensure that the horses are fine and, in general, are very ecologically minded souls. The seafood in this part of the world is outstanding—spot, sea mullet, croaker, flounder, gray trout, speckled trout, pompano, spanish mackerel, buefish, striped bass, red drum, king mackerel, and cobia—just to name a few.

This soup is my version of one we enjoy at a local café. I love the range of flavors—coconut milk, North Carolina yams, and hot chili peppers—complementing the local fish. It has a natural sweetness and is soothing. I think you will enjoy serving this to people who think they have tried it all.

Outer Banks Fish Chowder
Serves 4

2 cups *chicken* stock or vegetable stock
1 small, organic sweet onion, chopped
1 jalapeño pepper, seeded and chopped
2 medium *tomatoes*, seeded and chopped
2 medium organic yams, cut into 1/2-inch cubes
2 (8-ounce) cans unsweetened coconut milk
1 pound white fish, such as rockfish, tilapia, or bass
1/2 teaspoon sweet paprika
Sea salt
Freshly ground black pepper

Pour stock into a medium pot. Add onions, chili pepper, tomatoes, and yams. Cover and simmer for 10 minutes. Add coconut milk and fish; simmer for another 10 minutes. With a fork, gently break fish into bite-size pieces. Add paprika and season to taste with salt and pepper.

My best friend, Jane

4-wheel-drive vehicles on the beach of the Outer Banks, North Carolina, heading for home

Ever on the quest for fresh fruit and vegetables, friends and I came across the Vaughn Family Farm one lazy Sunday afternoon as we were driving around the farm area in southern Virginia Beach. This is one of the country's oldest family-owned farms, dating back to the 1600s. More idyllic-looking would be difficult to imagine.

The mother and her two daughters were at the rustic stand at the end of the road selling the family's produce. We could actually smell how sweet the melons were without even picking them up! The daughters were working for the summer, and the youngest said how much she would rather be riding horses that day. Her mum smiled and said, "If you want to ride, you're going to have to work too!" I thought, What great values to teach children in this day and age. The youngest daughter followed us out to our car to see our two dogs, Spirit and Riley, and to point to hers off in the distance by the barn. We smiled as we drove off, our trunk filled with fresh blueberries, blackberries, and melons to be made into our summer night's soup!

Chilled Melon Soup
Serves 4

1 large cantaloupe, chopped (about 4 cups)
1 tablespoon honey
Juice of 2 limes
2 tablespoons wine vinegar (white, if available)
Pinch of ground cardamom
1/4 cup chopped fresh mint leaves for garnish

Place melon in the bowl of food processor or in a blender. Add honey, lime juice, vinegar, and cardamom; blend until smooth. (You may need to divide the contents and blend this in two batches, depending on the size of your processor or blender.) Pour into glass bowl and chill for 4 to 5 hours. When ready to serve, garnish with fresh mint leaves.

This soup originated in Andalusia, Spain, where tomatoes are plentiful. This is a very simple, impressive-looking starter that takes very little time to prepare and requires no cooking. The colors are enhanced by the variety of vegetables used in making this chilled soup. Having a food processor or a blender, especially an immersion blender, allows you to make this a one-two-three-step dish.

To me, there is nothing more festive-looking than this yummy soup served in colorful bowls and garnished with an edible flower or two. Another suggestion is to garnish with whole wheat croutons or diced, hard-boiled eggs.

You will need 4 chilled soup cups or bowls

Andalusia Gazpacho
Serves 4

3 cloves garlic, peeled
4 slices whole wheat bread
2 cups chopped *red pepper*
1 cup chopped *yellow pepper*
7 large *vine-ripened tomatoes* (about 3 pounds), peeled
1 cup chopped sweet onion
6 tablespoons red wine vinegar
2 tablespoons extra virgin olive oil
2 teaspoons chervil
Sea salt
Freshly ground black pepper
1 cup whole wheat croutons for garnish (optional)
1 cup diced hard-boiled *egg* for garnish (optional)
Edible flowers for garnish (optional)

If using an immersion blender, place the garlic, bread, peppers, tomatoes, onions, vinegar, oil, and chervil in a large bowl; blend until smooth. Or place the ingredients in the bowl of a food processor or in a blender and blend until smooth. Season to taste with salt and pepper. If the mixture seems too thick, add a little cold water to make it soupy. Chill for a couple of hours.

Just before serving, place a couple of ice cubes in chilled soup cups and ladle the gazpacho over them. Garnish as desired.

Warm Your Soul Soups

I did not realize that most vegetarian chilies are made without an abundance of veggies until I started ordering vegetarian chili in restaurants. Sure, it did not contain ground meat, but where were the veggies? This creation is filled with vegetables, which will add dimension and great flavor to this nourishing and satisfying crowd pleaser. Vary the vegetables according to the season, always including as much fresh produce as possible.

You'll need to soak dried beans overnight before making recipe.

Vegetarian Chili—with the Veggies!
Serves 6-8

2 pounds dried kidney beans or 2 (18 ounce) cans kidney beans, drained and rinsed
5 tablespoons olive oil
2 medium yellow onions, roughly chopped
4 stalks celery, diced
5 cloves garlic, minced
28-ounce can whole tomatoes
28 ounces water
1 large sweet potato, diced
2 medium carrots, diced
1 medium zucchini, diced
1/4 pound green beans, stems removed and cut in half
2 teaspoons ground cumin
1 teaspoon ground coriander
1/2 teaspoon cayenne pepper (optional)
3 teaspoons sea salt
Whole grain tortilla chips (optional)

If using dried beans, cover them with ample water and let soak overnight. Drain and add fresh water to cover; cook on medium-high heat for approximately 30 minutes, until just tender. Do not overcook.

Meanwhile, heat oil in a large stockpot over medium-high heat. Add onions, celery, and garlic. Cook until translucent, about 10 minutes. Add remaining vegetables, spices, and seasonings; simmer for 15 minutes.

Once beans are cooked, drain and add to stockpot. Cover and cook for 1 hour and 30 minutes, stirring occasionally. Adjust seasoning to taste. Serve warm in large bowls, and top with organic whole grain tortilla chips.

Vegetarian Fare

"Eat your vegetables!" Don't you remember your mum or dad saying this when you were growing up? They were right on! Actually, 80 percent of our daily diet should be composed of alkaline-producing foods, which includes most vegetables and fruits as well as a few other foods. And that does not mean eating a huge, white baked potato with a ton of sour cream, butter, and bacon bits on it, either. Try to incorporate a variety of multi-hued vegetables into your diet. Color is not only pleasing to the eye, but it is healthy for your body.

There are so many wonderful ways to prepare vegetables. They can be simply steamed with only a dab of added butter, or fresh herbs can be incorporated to complement their smooth flavor. Cayce advised that when steaming vegetables, each type of vegetable should be steamed individually in patapar paper (unbleached parchment paper) or in a pressure cooker and the vitamin-rich juices retained. Well-cooked is the idea for vegetables served at dinner meals, according to Cayce, but not overcooked, so as not to destroy vitamins. (Raw vegetables are best to make up the noonday meal.)

You may want to try some of these ideas when preparing your vegetables. Pair fresh mint with butter beans, May peas, or cucumbers. Fresh sage adds a touch of elegance to butternut squash. My garden overflows with Italian basil to be added to summer salads and to make my favorite low-fat version of pesto. Sautéed mushrooms come alive with chopped, flat-leaf parsley. Try grilling corn on the cob, and instead of slathering it with butter, add finely chopped basil instead. It is delicious and much lower in fat. Za'Atar added to mashed potatoes or sweet potatoes is exotic and rich-tasting.

Each region of the world has its own special spices and herbs. By experimenting in the use of these with your vegetables, you can eliminate the overuse of salt, which is not recommended.

As a child, my plate was filled not with one vegetable, but an abundance of them. I am disappointed to go out and be served a dinner with only one or two vegetables. I want three or four to adorn my plate. It did help that my grandmother always had a vegetable garden. In my mind's eye, I see my sister Jennifer and myself sitting on Nanny's front steps, shelling peas for that evening's dinner, while she would be inside baking her homemade brown bread. We were spoiled with love and good food in our family. I can think of nothing more giving than preparing fresh vegetables for dinner for your family or anyone you love, including yourself!

My friends start teasing me around the end of June, when my very favorite butter beans are in season. I could eat them daily if left on my own. I don't suggest just eating one variety of vegetables, but trying them all. As I finish writing this book, I presently have a bushel of shelled butter beans reserved for me at a local farm.

The best place to get vegetables is in your garden, but not everyone has space for that. So, once again, support your local farmers and all the hard work they do in order to provide you with food. Cayce said to eat only locally grown, in-season vegetables. This makes so much sense, as who wants to go to the grocery store to buy vegetables shipped more than 5,000 miles that are no longer fresh? By the time they reach you, they are weeks old. By eating in-season vegetables indigenous to your area, you are allowing

your body to assimilate necessary vitamins and nutrients.

Many farmers markets now propose selling boxes of in-season vegetables weekly at a fixed price. What a joy to go pick up your fresh vegetables that have been picked that same day or the day before. The market cannot promise you what you will get, but at least you know it will be fresh! Many farms have a U-pick option, as well, which can save you a lot of money and make for a very pleasant outing. Another new trend is leasing plots of land to grow your own vegetables.

With the continued rise in cost of gasoline and economic decline, I feel more people are reverting to a healthier lifestyle. Instead of taking vacations far away from home, people are spending more time in their own vicinity. Driving to a local farm to pick one's own produce or to see cows and chickens is a great day-trip and a fun diversion.

My daughter Brooke lives in a condominium where each family is given a nice-size plot of land to grow their own vegetables. Most families have barbeque facilities as well, and the kids can roam around freely to enjoy the fresh air.

Once you get into the habit of eating locally grown, fresh vegetables, it will be a very difficult one to break. And once you get into the habit of replacing a mostly meat diet with mostly fresh vegetables and fruit, your health and vitality will soar to new heights. Cayce advised that only 20 percent of our diet be acid-producing, which includes meats—preferably fish, fowl, or lamb. As mentioned earlier, 80 percent of our diet should be alkaline-producing foods, mainly vegetables and fruits. Dried beans, tofu, and quinoa can be prepared in a lot of yummy ways to replace meat. Cayce also recommended that we eat more leafy green vegetables, more vegetables grown above the ground than below, and more nonstarchy vegetables than starchy.

In this chapter, you will find some very classic recipes, as well as some global ones, that incorporate herbs and spices. For every meat or fish casserole, there is a vegetarian one to replace it. Instead of Lancashire Lamb Hotpot, for example, why not Vegetarian Hotpot? Instead of Moroccan Chicken Tagine, why not try Moroccan Vegetable Tagine? Vegetarian Paella is one of my favorite recipes in this chapter, and people seem to love it whenever I make it. By making a double quantity of any casserole and freezing it, you'll have an entrée on hand for those days you may not feel like making anything.

Autumn Ratatouille
Vegetarian Paella
Tunisian Vegetarian Couscous
Vegetarian Hotpot
South African Spinach Quiche
Turkish Cabbage Dolma
Zucchini Risotto
Brooke's Grilled Eggplant
Indian Spiced Kale and Garbanzo Beans
Honey and Ginger Glazed Carrots
Wild Mushroom Ragout
Vegetable Stir Fry
Chop Suey
Stuffed Peppers with Wild Rice
Lentil Shepherd's Pie
Grilled Vegetables
Oven-Roasted Sweet Potatoes
Roasted Beets and Sautéed Beet Greens
Lebanese Mashed Potatoes

This vegetable dish is common in the Provence area of France, where eggplant, zucchini, and tomatoes grow in abundance. Herbes de Provence is the perfect complement to this earthy dish. Ratatouille is a wonderful Sunday night dinner. As it cooks, spend some time with your family. This dish can be served warm, or it is equally good served at room temperature, so it makes for great leftovers. Serve with a fresh green salad and hearty bread.

Autumn Ratatouille
Serves 8

3 tablespoons extra virgin olive oil
2 large Spanish onions (about 1 pound), diced
2 *sweet peppers* (about 1 pound), seeded and chopped
3 cloves garlic, minced
1 pound zucchini, diced
1 pound eggplant, diced
3 large (1 1/2 pounds) *tomatoes*, peeled and diced
2 teaspoons Herbes de Provence
Sea salt
Freshly ground black pepper
2 tablespoons chopped fresh parsley for garnish

Heat oil in a large pot over medium heat. Add onions and peppers; cook for approximately 5 minutes, until softened. Add garlic, zucchini, and eggplant; stir gently; cover. Simmer over medium heat for approximately 20 to 25 minutes, until vegetables are tender. Add tomatoes and Herbes de Provence; stir. Simmer over low heat, cover off, for approximately 5 minutes. Season to taste with salt and pepper. Garnish with parsley.

Vegetarian Fare

When my girls were very young, we drove from our home in Geneva to visit one of my best friends and her family in the Basque region of Northern Spain. Romina's parents did not speak one word of English, and we did not speak Spanish. I still get the giggles thinking about our "conversations." We managed to laugh every night at dinner and, of course, they adored my girls, as Spanish people tend to treat children like royalty.

While there, we ate fresh seafood paella, but this vegetarian version is equally tasty, using black olives, red peppers, zucchini, and garden peas to replace the typical fish. This is a one-dish meal that is cooked in a large wok or skillet. The saffron gives a beautiful aroma and color. I suggest using Spanish olive oil, which is an amber color and not as hearty as the Greek style, but any good quality, light variety of olive oil is a fine substitute. Typically, yellow rice is used, but brown rice makes for a heartier and healthier replacement. Once cooked, the paella can be served in the wok skillet or on a serving platter.

Vegetarian Paella
Serves 8

1/2 cup Spanish olive oil
2 1/2 cups brown rice
2 large onions (about 1 pound), diced
4 cloves garlic, minced
2 pinches of saffron strands
6 cups vegetable stock
1 teaspoon sea salt
1 teaspoon ground black pepper
3 medium zucchini (about 1 pound), diced
2 large *red peppers* (about 1 pound), diced
1 cup garden peas
1/2 cup cured olives, pit removed, for garnish
1/4 cup chopped parsley for garnish

Heat oil in a large wok or skillet. Add brown rice and onions; stir until rice is coated with oil. Add garlic, saffron strands, stock, sea salt, and pepper. Mix well, bringing just to boiling point; stir to distribute saffron. Arrange zucchini and red peppers on top of rice. Bring just to a boil; cover and simmer gently for approximately 40 minutes. Add peas and simmer with lid on for an additional 5 minutes. Just before serving, garnish with olives and chopped parsley.

Tunisia is a country many Europeans enjoy visiting on holiday. During one vacation, I stayed on an island called Djerba, where the architecture is striking. Homes, known as *menzels*, are all white with sky-blue, wrought-iron trimmings. The island is covered with more than a million date palms and 700,000 olive trees. Apricots, carobs, figs, grapes, grenadines, lemons, mandarins, oranges, and pomegranates also grow in abundance, and the taste of these fruits is sweet heaven. One feels at total peace here on the beautiful, azure blue Mediterranean Sea.

I had several favorite pastimes while on the island—galloping on horseback on the sandy white beaches, eating vegetable couscous almost daily, and looking for beautiful pottery made on the island. Apparently, I resemble a famous Tunisian singer named Sophie Sadek, because everywhere I went, the locals thought I was Sophie. It was hysterical. My friend was even offered a thousand camels by one merchant in exchange for me. Obviously, that did not happen, as I now live in Virginia.

The island is mostly inhabited by Berbers, so there are some similarities to the Moroccan cuisine. This vegetarian couscous is my rendition of food I tasted on this lovely island made famous by Homer's *Odyssey*. In Tunisia it is served with a very spicy sauce called *harissa*. My son-in-law Yann makes his own, but you can find it in the spice section of your grocery store or in Asian markets. I cook all the ingredients in one pot, contrary to the custom in Tunisia and Morocco. It just makes life easier! If you happen to have a large pottery serving platter, it would add authenticity to this festive meal.

Note: If using dried beans, you will need to soak them overnight before preparing recipe.

Tunisian Vegetarian Couscous
Serves 8

2 cups dried garbanzo beans or 4 (15-ounce) cans, drained
8 tablespoons butter
8 medium-size yellow onions (about 2 1/2 pounds), chopped
1/2 teaspoon turmeric
5 medium carrots (about 1 pound), cut into 1-inch lengths
3 medium zucchini (about 1 pound), cut into 1-inch lengths
1 pound green beans, cut into 1-inch lengths
1 teaspoon ground ginger
2 teaspoons ground cinnamon
3 cups vegetable stock
2 cups fresh or fresh-frozen diced pumpkin
4 pinches saffron, pulverized

Couscous
2 cups dry couscous
4 cups vegetable broth, heated
1 cup golden raisins
1 cup chopped dates
2 tablespoons butter

If using dried beans, soak overnight with sufficient water to cover completely. The next day, drain the garbanzo beans. Cover with fresh, cold water and 1 teaspoon of baking soda. Cook over medium heat with lid on for approximately one hour; drain.

Melt butter in a large pot over medium heat. Add onions and turmeric; cook gently until onions are translucent. Add garbanzo beans (canned beans should not be added at this point)), carrots, zucchini, green beans, ginger, cinnamon, and the 3 cups vegetable stock. Bring to a boil; reduce heat; cover and simmer for 30 minutes. Add pumpkin, saffron, and canned garbanzo beans, if using; cook an additional 20 minutes.

Meanwhile, place couscous in a medium-size bowl and cover with the 2 cups heated vegetable broth. Add raisins and dates; let sit for about 10 minutes, until couscous becomes tender and all liquid is absorbed. Transfer steamed couscous to a large serving platter. Add butter with a fork and smooth out any lumps.

Pour the vegetables, with liquid, over the couscous and serve at once.

Vegetarian Fare

Layers of colorful vegetables cooked slowly with layers of onions make for a very soothing dinner on any night of the week. Sweet potatoes or yams replace the white variety to add a natural sweetness. A side of steamed broccoli or Brussels sprouts adds color and nutrition to this yummy casserole.

Vegetarian Hotpot
Serves 4

16-ounce can peeled and *diced tomatoes*
1 teaspoon sea salt
1 teaspoon freshly ground black pepper
1 tablespoon dried thyme
4 large sweet *potatoes* (2 pounds), scrubbed, cut into 1/4-inch slices
1 large *red sweet pepper*, seeded, cut into 1/2-inch slices
1 large *yellow* or *orange sweet pepper*, seeded, cut into 1/2-inch slices
2 large yellow onions (about 1 pound), peeled, cut into 1/2-inch slices
3 tablespoons chopped parsley for garnish

Preheat oven to 300°. Butter a large ovenproof casserole dish. Add some of the tomatoes to line the bottom of the casserole. Cover with a bit of salt, pepper, and thyme. Put a layer of potatoes in the pan, a layer of red and yellow peppers, and a layer of onions; top with some of the tomato mixture. Repeat, ending with an extra layer of potatoes on top. Cover with foil and cook for 2 hours; remove foil for the last 15 minutes. Once top is browned, remove from oven and allow to rest for several minutes. Garnish with parsley, and serve.

My children are very fortunate to visit South Africa often. Their dad owns a gorgeous home in Wilderness, overlooking the Touw River Lagoon. Whenever my granddaughter Anais visits, she packs a suitcase full of her toys to distribute to children who have nothing or very little. She has done this of her own volition since she was five years old. Anais is a true humanitarian, and I feel very fortunate that she is a part of our family.

This dish was eaten by Bree, Anais and Luc on a recent safari at the camp where they were staying. I made it according to Bree's directions but decided to change the ingredients slightly to make it my own. Just as she said, it is absolutely creamy and dreamy. If you do not care for bacon, omit it or substitute turkey bacon. But if you do like bacon, ensure it is crisply cooked, as Cayce suggested.

This is a great luncheon treat or a light dinner served with a muscelin (spring mix) green salad and your choice of vinaigrette.

South African Spinach Quiche
Serves 4–6

10 ounces frozen *creamed spinach*
4 ounces *bacon* (optional)
1 tablespoon olive oil (if omitting bacon)
1/2 cup chopped onions
6 *eggs*
1 cup heavy *cream*
1 cup grated *cheddar cheese*
8 ounces chopped *feta cheese*
2 teaspoons baking powder
Sea salt
Freshly ground black pepper
1 frozen whole wheat pie crust

Preheat oven to 350°. Cook spinach according to package directions; drain and squeeze out extra liquid.

If using bacon, cook until crisp; crumble; blot on paper towels. Add onions to skillet and sauté until well browned. Cool to room temperature.

If omitting bacon, heat olive oil over medium-high heat; stir in onions and sauté until well browned. Cool to room temperature.

In a medium-size bowl, whisk eggs until well beaten. Add cream, cheddar, feta, and baking powder. Season with salt and pepper. Stir in spinach, onions, and bacon, if using. Pour filling into frozen pie shell. Bake for 30 to 35 minutes, until golden brown on top and mixture is firm. Let stand for 10 minutes before cutting into serving pieces.

Lioness in South Africa

Vegetarian Fare

Anyone who has traveled to Turkey (or Greece) will have experienced some form of dolma. However, cabbage replaces the normal grape leaves here. And instead of white rice, there is brown rice, which lends a nuttier texture. Chestnuts can be found in glass jars in the produce section of your supermarket. Black currants and toasted pine nuts add their respective sweet and savory flavors to make for an elegant meal. This dish will surprise your family and friends in its complexity. It takes a bit of time to make but will be well worth your patience. This recipe is based on one from daughter Bree's colleague's at Procter and Gamble in Geneva, and I thank her.

Turkish Cabbage Dolma
Serves 6

1 large white cabbage (about 2 pounds)
1 tablespoon sea salt
2 tablespoons olive oil
4 onions (approximately 1 1/2 pounds), minced
1 cup *tomato sauce*
1 pound chestnuts
1/4 cup toasted pine nuts
1/4 cup black currants
2 cups brown rice
4 cups boiling water
1/2 teaspoon dried cumin
1/4 cup water
Boiling water
Lemon slices for garnish
Fresh parsley sprig for garnish

Remove core of cabbage with a sharp knife; pour sea salt into the hole. Submerge cabbage in a pot of boiling water; cook for 5 to 6 minutes; drain. Allow cabbage to cool sufficiently that you can easily separate the leaves. Place leaves one by one on a large plate.

In a medium pot, heat olive oil over medium heat; add onions; cook for 3 minutes, until translucent. Add tomato sauce, chestnuts, toasted pine nuts, and black currants; stir.

Meanwhile, place rice in a separate bowl; pour the 4 cups boiling water over rice; let sit for 10 minutes. Drain water; add rice to onion mixture. Add cumin and the 1/4 cup water; cover; simmer over medium-high heat for approximately 10 minutes. Let cool.

To prepare dolma, lay pieces of cabbage on flat work surface. Each leaf will be different, depending on its size, so add just enough rice mixture that you can adequately fold the leaf around it. To roll the cabbage leaves, start by folding the side edges of the leaf in first, then roll. Carefully place dolma in a large pot, and on top of each other as necessary. Fill pot half full with boiling water; simmer over medium-low heat for 30 minutes. Transfer dolma to a serving plate to cool. Garnish with fresh lemon slices and sprigs of parsley.

Every summer, my granddaughter Anais comes to visit me in Virginia to go to surf camp and to enjoy the beautiful weather, the ocean and, of course, her Nana. In 2005 her Swiss grandmother, my friend Jacqueline, came to stay with us for a week of sun and fun. Unfortunately for her, that year the weather played havoc on us and it rained almost every day of her short visit. So we did what we both love to do and cooked. Jacqueline is Swiss Italian and taught me how to make risotto the authentic way, which means a half hour of constant stirring. There is no other way to make this creamy delight, and I would not suggest the no-stir method, as it will not be the texture it should be and will not really be risotto at all.

While stirring, you can entertain your guests in lively conversation, sing or listen to them or, if alone, go into a cooking meditative state! Vegetable stock can easily replace the white wine in this dish. For best results, use freshly grated Parmesan cheese if your pocketbook allows.

This is an outstanding meal served with a fresh green salad. Most people will appreciate the tender, loving care put into making this!

Zucchini Risotto
Serves 4-6

3 tablespoons unsalted *butter*
1 small onion, finely chopped
3/4 pound zucchini, chopped
2 cups Arborio rice
1/2 cup dry white wine
6 cups vegetable stock
2 tablespoons unsalted *butter*
1 cup freshly grated *Parmesan cheese*
White pepper (optional)
Zucchini flowers for garnish

Heat 6 cups vegetable stock to boiling. Meanwhile, in a deep pot, melt butter over medium heat; add onion and zucchini; sauté for 10 minutes. Add rice and stir until coated with butter. Pour in wine and cook until it evaporates, stirring constantly. Add boiling vegetable stock a half cup at a time, stirring constantly. This step is very important: allow liquid to be absorbed before adding more vegetable stock. After about 15 minutes, the rice will become the consistency of porridge. At this point, add butter, Parmesan cheese, and pepper, if desired. Cover risotto and let sit for several minutes before serving.

If you have access to zucchini flowers, use them as a garnish for this dish.

Variation: Garden peas or asparagus can replace zucchini.

Vegetarian Fare

This side dish comes to me from my eldest daughter, Brooke, and incorporates a myriad of flavors. Brooke lives in a fantasy-like medieval village called Coppet, situated fifteen minutes from Geneva on Lake Geneva. There is a typically immaculate farm within walking distance of her home where she buys most of her produce. The Swiss are fastidious and pragmatic people, as they do not have much land, and every inch is utilized amazingly. I am not kidding when I say that most Swiss farms are as neat as most upscale clothing stores! Everything has its place.

I am proud of both my daughters for many reasons, but mainly because they love to cook. They have great careers as well as small families. However, every night around 7 o'clock, they sit down with their respective families to a home-cooked meal. My son-in-law Yann is also a wonderful cook and helps Brooke in the kitchen often.

While raising your children, do try to share mealtime together. Trust me, no matter how busy they are, they will repeat this wonderful habit when they grow up! And then . . . you can visit them and taste their cooking creations. Brooke served grilled chicken, pineapple, and couscous with this amazing dish.

Brooke's Grilled Eggplant
Serves 2

1 Japanese eggplant
Splash of extra virgin olive oil
3 tablespoons black olive tapenade
8-ounce log soft *goat cheese,* cut into 4 slices

Preheat oven to 350°. Cut eggplant in half lengthwise. If you cannot find a thin eggplant, then cut a big portion out of the middle of a larger one, as you do not want the eggplant to be too thick.

Pour a splash of olive oil in a medium frying pan (or just use a grill), and lightly grill/cook the eggplant on each side. Remove eggplant from pan or grill and place skin side down in an ovenproof dish. Spread tapenade on eggplant; top with goat cheese. Bake in the oven until cheese is bubbly and lightly browned. It's ready!

Swiss Cows

Family dinner in Geneva, Switzerland

Cumin, coriander, and garam masala are typical spices found in Indian cuisine. They add smoke and earthiness to anything they accompany. I have never been to India, but I have eaten in many Indian restaurants in England while living there and learned to love these spices.

Kale is a leafy green vegetable that belongs to the Brassica family, a group of vegetables including cabbage, collards, and Brussels sprouts. Garbanzo beans are high in protein, so this dish is a perfect accompaniment to any vegetarian platter.

Indian Spiced Kale and Garbanzo Beans
Serves 4

1 tablespoon olive oil
3 cloves garlic, crushed
1 pound kale, stems removed, chopped
1 cup vegetable broth or water
1 teaspoon dried coriander
4 cups boiling water
1/2 teaspoon dried cumin
1/4 teaspoon garam masala
1/4 teaspoon sea salt (optional)
1 (8-ounce) can garbanzo beans, drained and rinsed

Heat oil over medium heat in a large skillet. Add garlic and sauté for 1 to 3 minutes, careful not to brown. Add kale, broth, coriander, cumin, garam masala, and salt to pan. Stir occasionally until cooked, about 10 minutes. Stir in garbanzo beans and cook for 1 to 2 minutes more.

Vegetarian Fare

This is one of those vegetables your mum always said to eat, and she was right. Carrots are an excellent source of vitamin A, among other things. Carrots are available year-round, but they are at their best when in season, during the summer and fall. There is nothing quite like a baby carrot pulled from the earth, because it tastes so sweet.

This is a recipe my mum used often when cooking Sunday dinners. It is a great accompaniment to roasts or savory dishes, such as Lentil Shepherd's Pie (page 112). I like the carrots to have a slightly glazed caramel appearance.

Honey and Ginger Glazed Carrots
Serves 4

2 pounds carrots, peeled and julienned
2-inch piece fresh ginger, peeled and minced
1 tablespoon freshly squeezed lemon juice
1 teaspoon grated lemon zest
2 tablespoons *butter*
2 tablespoons honey
Fresh chopped parsley for garnish

Place carrots and ginger in a large saucepan. Partially cover with water; bring to a boil. Simmer carrots for approximately 8 to 10 minutes, stirring occasionally. Once water has evaporated, add lemon juice, lemon zest, butter, and honey; cook over medium heat for several minutes, until the carrots are shining with glaze. Garnish with parsley. Serve immediately.

This comforting and nutty blend is mouthwatering for any mushroom lover. Many people collect their own mushrooms in the wild, which is not suggested unless you really know your varieties, because mushrooms can be highly toxic, even lethal.

Pharmacies in Switzerland will identify edible wild mushrooms for you. It does look rather odd, but you will often see people walking into these pharmacies carrying a basketful. In days gone by in Italy, the government paid experts to sit at a table in the town center to instruct people on the art of finding nonpoisonous varieties. But here in America, farmers markets and many grocery stores carry a wide range of mushrooms in their produce department. Once bought, mushrooms should be cooked fairly quickly, as they do not store well. To clean mushrooms, take a damp paper towel and rub off any dirt.

Serve this ragout with toasted whole wheat crostini, or serve with an arugula salad, shaved Parmesan, a sprinkling of fresh lemon juice and olive oil, and you have a very Italian-inspired lunch!

Wild Mushroom Ragout
Serves 4-6

2 tablespoons *butter*
1 tablespoon olive oil
2 cloves garlic, crushed
1 large shallot, finely diced
1 pound mushrooms—porcini, oyster, chanterelles, or borel, roughly chopped
1 tablespoon chopped fresh thyme
2 tablespoons lemon juice

Melt butter in a medium sauté pan on medium heat; add olive oil and mix well. Add garlic and shallot to pan; cook for 1 to 2 minutes. Add mushrooms; turn heat to medium high and cook for 3 minutes. Add fresh thyme and lemon juice; stir. Remove from heat and serve over whole wheat crostinis or wild rice.

Vegetarian Fare

For those of you who have extremely busy lives and don't seem to find the time to cook, perhaps take an hour one day of each week to wash, chop, slice, and store bags of fresh vegetables to have on hand. Although it is certainly better to wash and chop vegetables just before using, having them on hand will ensure that you can still make a great-tasting dinner in no time at all. Actually, I recommend getting your family or loved ones involved in this process. The more time you spend together doing healthy and satisfying activities, the better off you will be.

Stir-fry vegetables are not fried but stirred over high heat quickly. Always cook the hardest vegetables first, then the softest ones at the end. Any combination works and the more fresh veggies you use, the better you will feel. Add tofu for protein, if you like. Organic brown rice is a great accompaniment, as well.

Vegetable Stir Fry
Serves 4

1 tablespoon sunflower oil
1 cup sliced onions
1 cup sliced *red pepper*
2 cloves garlic, minced
1 cup sliced carrots
1 cup broccoli florets
1 cup snow peas
1 cup sliced button mushrooms
1 cup sliced zucchini
1 tablespoon low-sodium soy sauce
1/4 teaspoon cayenne pepper (optional)
Chopped fresh parsley for garnish

In a large wok or skillet, heat oil over medium-high heat. Add onions, red pepper, and garlic; cook for 3 to 4 minutes, stirring occasionally. Add carrots and broccoli; continue to cook for 3 to 4 minutes, until tender crisp.

Add snow peas, mushrooms, and zucchini; cook until liquid from mushrooms is absorbed. Stir vegetables often so they do not stick to the pan. Add soy sauce and cayenne pepper, if using. Garnish with parsley and serve immediately.

Chop Suey is usually made with leftover vegetables, which is how it got its name, meaning "a little of this and a little of that." It is one dish surely found in all American Chinese restaurants. I am including this dish because it is an easy weeknight dinner and a great way to use up fresh vegetables. Children actually love this and it is usually served over steamed white rice. I suggest using brown or wild rice.

Chop Suey
Serves 4

1 tablespoon sesame oil
1 teaspoon sunflower oil
2 small white onions, sliced
1 clove garlic, minced
1 stalk *celery,* sliced diagonally
1 cup coarsely shredded cabbage
1 cup diagonally sliced carrots
1 cup cauliflower florets
1 cup broccoli florets
1 cup sliced water chestnuts, drained
2 cups crunchy bean sprouts
2 tablespoons low-sodium soy sauce

In a wok or a large frying pan, heat the oils over medium-high heat. Add onions, garlic, and celery; cook for 2 to 3 minutes. Add cabbage, carrots, cauliflower, and broccoli to wok or pan. Stir constantly and cook for approximately 10 minutes, or until vegetables are just tender. Add water chestnuts, bean sprouts, and soy sauce; cook for 1 to 2 minutes. Serve immediately.

Vegetarian Fare

Mostly, one will find that peppers are stuffed with white rice or orzo in Mediterranean countries. I wanted to create a healthier version of this dish, and this is what I came up with. It abounds with flavor. The wild rice adds a nutty flavor and texture. These delicious stuffed peppers will be a great addition to any vegetarian platter, accompanied with humus and a Greek salad.

Stuffed Peppers with Wild Rice
Serves 4

2 cups cooked wild rice
1 cup toasted pine nuts
1/2 cup golden raisins
1/2 teaspoon minced fresh rosemary
1 teaspoon freshly ground black pepper
4 medium-size *red bell peppers*, halved lengthwise, seeded
2 cups vegetable stock
8 ounces crumbled *feta* (optional)
Fresh rosemary sprigs for garnish
Lemon wedges for garnish

Preheat oven to 350°. In a medium-size bowl, mix cooked rice, pine nuts, raisins, rosemary, and pepper. Mound pepper halves with rice mixture, dividing equally. Arrange in an ovenproof baking dish; add vegetable stock to the dish. Bake peppers uncovered until tops are browned, approximately 1 hour. Top with feta cheese and broil until melted, about 2 minutes. Transfer peppers to platter and serve immediately. Garnish serving platter or individual plates with rosemary sprigs and lemon wedges.

Shepherd's pie, made with either ground lamb or ground beef or both, was often on the menu when I was growing up, and I loved it. By substituting lentils, this becomes a vegetarian dish that is still packed with lots of protein. Sweet potatoes add much-needed color and bulk. This is definitely a comfort food recipe, and it freezes well, too, if there are any leftovers. A plain herbed salad goes well with this delicious dish.

Note: the sweet potatoes can be baked a day ahead.

Lentil Shepherd's Pie
Serves 8

2 cups dried brown or French lentils
4 cups water
2 tablespoons olive oil
2 large Spanish onions, peeled and chopped
2 cloves garlic, minced
4 stalks celery, chopped
4 carrots, chopped
4 ounces tomato puree
1 cup water
2 teaspoons Herbes de Provence
2 pounds sweet potatoes, mashed
4 tablespoons butter

Preheat oven to 375°. Pour lentils into large saucepan; cover with water. Bring to a boil; cover. Simmer over low heat for 45 minutes, until tender.

Meanwhile, in a large skillet, heat olive oil over medium heat. Add onions, garlic, celery, and carrots; cook until just tender. Add cooked lentils, tomato puree, water, and herbs. Stir and continue cooking for several minutes, until mixture is well blended.

Place cooked lentil and tomato mixture in a lightly oiled, medium-size, ovenproof baking dish. Cover with mashed sweet potatoes. Put dabs of butter on top of potatoes; cook approximately 45 to 50 minutes, until golden brown. Remove from oven and wait 10 minutes before serving.

Vegetarian Fare

If you are lucky enough to have a gas barbeque, then grilling vegetables this way will fast become a favorite. There are great slotted, stainless steel grilling pans that are used just for grilling vegetables, and they are well worth the small expense. This allows you to watch the vegetables and stir when necessary. If you do not have a grilling pan, then wrap the vegetables in foil and place them on the grill. Any combination of your favorite veggies can be used, but these are the ones that seem to go well for me. You can either make a meal of this, or serve it as a side dish with grilled fish, lamb, or chicken. If there are any leftovers, chill them and add them to a green salad for a yummy lunch another day.

Grilled Vegetables
Serves 4

1/2 pound red onions, quartered
3 cloves garlic, minced
1/2 pound zucchini, sliced lengthwise in 4-inch strips
1/2 pound yellow squash, sliced lengthwise in 4-inch strips
1/2 pound carrots, peeled, sliced lengthwise in 4-inch strips
1/2 pound portobello mushrooms, sliced
2 tablespoons olive oil
1 tablespoon freshly squeezed lemon juice
2 teaspoons Herbes de Provence
Sea salt
Freshly ground black pepper
Chopped flat-leaf parsley for garnish

Preheat grill to medium heat, approximately 300°, or allow coals to burn down to white ash. In a large mixing bowl, add vegetables, olive oil, lemon juice, Herbes de Provence, and seasonings; mix well. Marinate for 30 minutes to enhance flavor. Place vegetables on top of grilling basket and distribute evenly. Put cover over grill. Cook for 30 to 40 minutes, stirring occasionally, until desired doneness. Garnish with parsley and serve immediately.

Grilling vegetables in Monaco

Sweet potato slices, baked in the oven with garlic and cayenne pepper, are absolutely delicious. With a little squeeze of fresh lime juice and chopped chives for the garnish, an additional dimension is added. These are delicious served with roast chicken and sweet peas.

Oven-Roasted Sweet Potatoes
Serves 4

1 pound sweet *potatoes*, scrubbed, sliced 1 inch thick
3 cloves garlic, thinly sliced
1 tablespoon olive oil
1/2 teaspoon cayenne pepper (optional)
1 tablespoon freshly squeezed lime juice
2 teaspoons chopped fresh chives

Preheat oven to 400°. Line a baking sheet with unbleached parchment paper. Meanwhile, in a mixing bowl, mix sweet potatoes, garlic, olive oil, and cayenne pepper. Place mixture on prepared baking sheet; bake approximately 30 minutes, turning once after 15 minutes. Check for doneness. Place potatoes on serving platter; drizzle with lime juice and sprinkle with chives.

Vegetarian Fare

On a recent outing to a nearby farm in Pungo, Virginia, my friend Jane and I stopped at the beautiful 167-acre Cromwell Farm to buy our dinner vegetables. There we were greeted by a lovely family, consisting of mum, dad, daughter, and son. We spied some wonderful-looking beets, but the greens had been chopped off. When we said we love beets but wanted the greens, the kids beckoned us to follow them. Off to the fields we went with their dog, Mag, shadowing our every move. Much to our delight, they pulled up fresh beets and greens straight from the earth. The family was so excited to share their love for farming and wanted to know how we prepared our greens.

When we got home that night, all we could talk about was this wonderful family of farmers and their dedication to supplying healthy food to the local community. So this recipe is in honor of them, to show our gratitude for their hard work. It must be very difficult to get up at the crack of dawn to care for the gardens and to gladly be at their charming stand—made with recycled barn wood—to sell their wares day in and day out during picking season. The beets and greens were outstanding!

Roasted Beets and Sautéed Beet Greens
Serves 4

Roasted Beets
2 pounds fresh beets
2 tablespoons olive oil
1 tablespoon sea salt

Preheat oven to 400°. Remove beet greens at the stem, being careful not to cut into the beet, as this will cause bleeding when cooking; reserve beet greens. Wash beets thoroughly, scrubbing off stems and earth; pat dry. Roll beets in olive oil; pat with sea salt. Wrap beets individually in foil. Place on a baking sheet and bake in oven for approximately 1 hour. Partially remove foil from one beet. Insert a toothpick into the center to check if done; it should go in easily. Once tender, take beets out of foil and remove skin by running under cold water. Serve warm with butter or chilled in a salad.

Sautéed Beet Greens
2 large handfuls of beet greens (about 1 pound)
1 tablespoon olive oil
1 tablespoons minced garlic
1 tablespoon chopped fresh herbs of choice
1/2 teaspoon sea salt
1/2 teaspoon freshly ground black pepper

Wash beet greens thoroughly to remove sand. Typically, you will have to wash 3 to 4 times. Remove leaves from stems and discard stems; pat leaves dry.

Heat olive oil in a large skillet over medium-high heat. Add minced garlic and greens. Stir and cook for 4 minutes, or until greens are wilted. Do not overcook or you will lose the vitamins. Sprinkle with fresh herbs of your choice, sea salt, and pepper. Serve immediately.

Choosing fresh produce for tonight's dinner!

The Lebanese certainly have a flare for healthy and great-tasting food. Instead of putting butter and cream on their mashed potatoes, they add freshly squeezed lemon juice, olive oil, and za'atar. It is a smashing combination and exudes an incredible taste I hope you will try. Cayce did suggest omitting the pulp from white potatoes, but he also emphasized that exceptions can sometimes be made in life. But be sure to buy organic when using white potatoes.

Lebanese Mashed Potatoes
Serves 4

6-8 medium Yukon gold *potatoes*, peeled and quartered
1/3 cup olive oil
1/3 cup fresh lemon juice
3 cloves garlic, minced
1 teaspoon sea salt
2 tablespoons chopped fresh mint for garnish

Cook potatoes in a large pot of boiling water until tender, approximately 15 minutes. Drain well and mash until smooth. Add olive oil, lemon juice, garlic, and sea salt. Garnish with fresh mint.

From the Seas and Rivers

By eating fish several times a week, you will be including a wonderful source of protein in your diet. Doctors today cannot emphasize enough how beneficial Omega 3's (found especially in salmon, mackerel, sardines, and shellfish) are to strengthening our hearts and adding to our total well-being. Consuming these foods is associated with low cholesterol and low LDL (the bad one) levels.

Try to eat local fish not only for its health benefits but also for the ecological reasons I repeat over and over. It is not always possible to buy fish caught close to your home, but do try. One does have to use a little caution when buying fresh fish in the market. If buying a whole fish, be sure the eyes are clear. If the eyes are cloudy, the fish was probably harvested more than five days earlier. The flesh should be firm but spring back when touched. Ask to smell the fish you are buying. If it is pungent, then put it back and ask for something fresher. There should not be a strong odor. Fish is not like wine. It does not improve with age.

The diet in Mediterranean countries is rich in the consumption of fish, fruits, nuts, whole grains, legumes, vegetables, wine, and olive oil. This way of eating is associated with longer life and less heart disease as well as protection against some cancers. Cayce's diet suggestions are compatible with this diet. He said that eating seafood at least once or twice a week, especially clams, oysters, shrimp, or lobster, would supply necessary elements, such as calcium and phosphorous, for our bodies. Modern science supports many of these same suggestions for optimum health. Cayce also recommended eating the bones found in canned fish because of the high calcium content. It was suggested that oysters or clams be consumed raw, and the others roasted or boiled and seasoned with butter. (275-24)

As a child, and to this day, I loved fish for dinner—whole wild salmon barbequed on my grandmother's grill, raw oysters, steamed clams, steamed lobster, grilled river trout, and fresh fish cakes—and shad roe for breakfast. When I lived in Jeddah, Saudi Arabia, on the Red Sea, my favorite fish was Red Sea snapper, which I ate often. It is a sweet-tasting fish that I even ate cold for breakfast if I felt I needed protein. Squid could be caught easily there, as well. Instead of frying it, gently sautéing it in olive oil and fresh lemon juice gives the purest and crispest of flavors of that incredible creature.

Children in America, especially, are often introduced to fish in the form of a heavily breaded and fried stick; this is totally unhealthy. In this section, I have chosen some of my favorite versions to cook fish that are also child friendly. Encourage your children to try new tastes, and once again, the earlier you do this, the better. Fish tacos are an amusing way to do so. What child does not love peanut butter, and it is incorporated in this recipe. Also, kids love color in their food, and in the rainbow hues of Asian Slaw, you have achieved this aspect.

Canadian Seafood Newburg
Lopez Island Fish Tacos
Grilled Salmon with Blueberry Coulis
Poached Salmon with Remoulade
Baked Halibut with Parsley Butter
Grilled Tuna with Lemon Marinade
Lake Geneva Perch Filets
Asian Shrimp Skewers and Peanut Sauce
Mediterranean Fish Kabobs
Flounder with Pesto Sauce
Seafood Quesadillas
Shrimp Pad Thai
White Fish with Mushroom Sauce
Asian Salmon Cakes
Steamed Mussels in Wine

This is a great first cousin to the very famous Lobster Newburg, which is one of my favorite dishes. Few of us have access to fresh lobster, and Seafood Newburg is a more economical version, as well. By using the same seasonings and replacing lobster with reasonably priced fish, I think most people will enjoy this robust casserole. Serve with organic basmati brown rice and a green salad. Any leftovers will be even better the second day. This is also a great casserole for casual entertaining, with very little fuss.

Canadian Seafood Newburg
Serves 6

1/4 cup unsalted *butter*
1/4 cup unbleached flour
1 1/2 cups *milk* or rice milk
1/2 cup chopped onion
2 tablespoons chopped fresh parsley
1 teaspoon dry mustard
1 teaspoon dried dill
2 tablespoons lemon juice
1/4 cup dry sherry
2 teaspoons Worcestershire sauce
1 pound large shrimp, shelled and deveined
1/2 pound lump crabmeat
1 large can (16 ounces) tuna chunks with oil

Topping
3 tablespoons *butter,* melted
1 cup panko (Japanese bread crumbs)

Preheat oven to 375°. Grease a 2-quart ovenproof casserole; set aside.

Melt butter in a large saucepan over medium heat, and whisk in the flour to make a roux. Gradually add milk, stirring constantly so as not to form lumps. Stir until thickened; remove from heat. Add onions, parsley, mustard, dill, lemon juice, sherry, and Worcestershire sauce to roux; stir. Stir in shrimp, crabmeat, and tuna. Pour mixture into prepared pan.

For the topping, mix together melted butter and panko. Spread evenly on top of fish mixture. Bake in oven for approximately 25 minutes, or until golden brown on top.

In 1999, my dog, Dinky, and I drove across America, to live on Lopez Island in the uppermost section of Washington State. As anyone who remembers Dinky will tell you, he was a warrior in a Cairn Terrier's body. I have never had a dog like him in my life and still dream of him years later.

The trip was quite an adventure. My friends and children could not believe I was driving across the country, because I do not even know how to read a map! I can still see Brooke standing in her driveway, eyes brimming with tears, as Dinky and I pulled away with my car packed to the gills. Brooke made us each picnics to last several days and made sure Dinky had a resting space in both the back and front seats. Well, I never knew where we would stop for the night and just had to rely on my faith that we would find a motel that would accept a dog. A separate book would have to be written of the Bobbie and Dinky adventures.

Once we rested after our record-breaking drive of five days, I started working in a friend's small restaurant called the Bay Café. There I learned many new ideas about food. It was the best restaurant on the island. Actually, there were only four restaurants on this piece of land, 10 miles long and 5 miles wide, but that did not diminish the fact that great locally grown and organic creations were served at the Bay for outstanding creations.

There was an airstrip the size of a football field that reminded me of one in an Indiana Jones adventure film. Sometimes I was sent there to collect the Alaskan halibut and salmon flown in for the restaurant. I had no idea how large and heavy these fish could be until I had to lift a box of one into my car.

At the Bay, only locally grown organic produce and edible flowers were used. One of my favorite dishes served there was a version of this fresh fish taco with Asian slaw and peanut sauce. I do not imagine everyone has access to fresh Alaskan halibut, so any firm, white fish will be fine in this recipe. And if you cannot buy fresh fish, use a good quality frozen one instead. Everyone loves this recipe, because the tacos can be assembled however you like!

Lopez Island Fish Tacos
Serves 4

8 Taco shells
1 tablespoon sunflower oil
1 pound fresh halibut
2 cups Asian Slaw (page 51)
4 tablespoons peanut sauce (see Indonesian Chicken Satay, page 150)

Preheat oven to 350°. Place taco shells on baking sheet. Bake for 5 minutes, or until crisp. Meanwhile, put 1 tablespoon sunflower oil in a medium-size skillet. Once heated, add halibut; cook for 3 to 4 minutes on each side. Fish should be flaky but not dry.

Place taco shells on serving platter. Add 1/4 cup Asian Slaw to each shell. Add halibut. Drizzle with heated peanut sauce. Serve at once.

Road trip with Dinky

Salmon and blueberries complement each other and make for a beautifully hued plate. The combination may sound unusual, but it is typical of the Pacific Northwestern way of presenting this healthy fish. Grilling salmon on cedar planks lends a smoky taste. You can buy untreated cedar planks at your local hardware store. Soak them in water for at least 1 to 24 hours before placing on your grill.

Blueberries are full of antioxidants. If you cannot find fresh ones, use the frozen variety. The sweetness of the blueberry coulis melts in your mouth.

Grilled Salmon with Blueberry Coulis
Serves 4

Blueberry Coulis
1 pint (2 cups) blueberries, rinsed
1/2 cup maple syrup
1/2 cup Dijon mustard
2 tablespoons red wine vinegar
1/2 teaspoon freshly ground black pepper (optional)

Cook ingredients over medium-high heat for 15 minutes, stirring occasionally. Keep warm until ready to serve. (The coulis can be stored in the refrigerator for several days before making this dish. If refrigerated, reheat slowly.)

4 king salmon steaks (about 8 ounces each)
1/2 cup olive oil
Juice and zest of 1 lemon
Sea salt
Freshly ground black pepper

Wash salmon thoroughly and pat dry with paper towels. Place two salmon steaks on each plank. Mix together olive oil, lemon juice, and zest in a small bowl. Brush each steak with mixture. Season to taste with salt and pepper. Place planks on preheated grill (or gas grill temperature set at 375°). Bake for approximately 8 to 10 minutes, or until steaks are firm to the touch.

Remove salmon from planks with a metal spatula and place on serving platter. Serve with blueberry coulis and drizzle over salmon.

My friends always ask me to make poached salmon, thinking it is the best they have ever eaten. In reality, I was brought up with this low-fat way of cooking salmon, a painless way to prepare this Omega-3-rich fish, and very satisfying served with remoulade. This French sauce resembles tartar sauce and is easy to assemble, highly complementary, and does not overwhelm the fresh taste of salmon. The salmon is equally great served right out of the oven or refrigerated and paired with chilled asparagus.

Poached Salmon with Remoulade
Serves 8

Remoulade
1 cup mayonnaise
2 tablespoons chopped mixed herbs—parsley, chives, and tarragon
1 tablespoon chopped capers
1 teaspoon anchovy paste

Mix ingredients together; cover and refrigerate until ready to use. Store in a glass jar in the refrigerator for up to 3 days.

1 salmon filet (about 4 pounds), skin removed
2 tablespoons grain mustard
Sea salt
Cracked black pepper
2 teaspoons dried dill
2 lemons, sliced into rounds
Lemon wedges and fresh dill sprigs for garnish

Preheat oven to 350°. Wash salmon thoroughly and pat dry with paper towels. Place whole salmon filet in a large ovenproof dish . Slather on mustard. Season with salt, pepper, and dill. Fill pan with water until it comes just halfway up the fish. Add lemon slices, some on top of salmon and some in water, and bake for approximately 20 minutes. Allow fish to cool in its poaching liquids for at least 10 minutes; gently, with two spatulas, place salmon on serving platter. Garnish with lemon wedges and fresh dill sprigs. Serve with remoulade.

Variation: Use dry white wine instead of water to poach salmon.

Halibut has to be one of the tastiest fish in the ocean. It is a white fish and does not have a meaty flavor, like mackerel or any of the darker fish. Baking anything takes the pain out of cleanup and mess, especially when you use parchment paper.

Just the simple touch of adding parsley butter and fresh lemon to this buttery-tasting fish makes it elegant fare for a party or for family. For a colorful and healthy plate, serve with oven-baked sweet potatoes with lots of butter, garden peas, and steamed yellow squash. Note that in reading 1342-1, it was suggested that "roasted yams or sweet potatoes are very good if plenty of butter is taken with same." That makes me happy because I happen to love butter. The parsley butter can be made several days in advance.

Baked Halibut with Parsley Butter
Serves 4

Garlic and Parsley Butter
2 cloves garlic, minced
1 bunch flat-leaf parsley, stems removed
8 tablespoons unsalted *butter,* room temperature
1/4 teaspoon cracked black pepper

Place all ingredients in a food processor; pulse for 20 to 30 seconds, until well blended

2-pound halibut filet
2 tablespoons olive oil
Sea salt
Cracked black pepper
2 tablespoons garlic and parsley *butter*

Preheat oven to 400°. Line a baking sheet with parchment paper. Wash halibut thoroughly; pat dry with paper towels; place halibut on prepared baking sheet. Brush with olive oil, sea salt, and black pepper. Bake for 20 minutes, turning once. Plate the fish and top with two tablespoons of garlic/parsley butter. Serve immediately.

From the Seas and Rivers

Once again, living by the Atlantic Ocean has its advantages. I remember a neighbor arriving at my North End house one day with tuna that had just been caught. It was so fresh it could have been eaten raw, like sushi. Instead, I marinated it in my favorite citrus vinaigrette for 10 minutes and then grilled it on the barbeque so it was seared on the outside and pink on the inside. Delicious is an understatement.

Not everyone likes tuna cooked this way, so you will have to do to your own liking. I do recommend getting your grill very hot so that there will be sear marks if you like it rare! I feel that overcooking tuna makes it dry. But, suit yourself.

Tuna is great served with a large muscelin greens salad, baked sweet potatoes, and steamed green beans.

Grilled Tuna with Lemon Marinade
Serves 4

1 1/2 pounds sashimi-grade tuna steak
1/4 cup Bree's Citrus Vinaigrette (page 59)
2 tablespoons Herbes de Provence
Chopped fresh herbs, lemon wedges, and pitted Kalamata olives for garnish

Place tuna, vinaigrette, and herbs in a gallon-size freezer bag or mixing bowl. Make sure the tuna is coated with the marinade. Seal the bag or cover the bowl. Refrigerate for no longer than 20 minutes.

When grill is hot, add the tuna steaks, turning only once, and cook until desired doneness.

Garnish with chopped fresh herbs, lemon wedges, and pitted Kalamata olives.

Virginia Beach, Virginia, Oceanfront

Lake Geneva, or Lac Lemain, is the largest freshwater lake in Western Europe. The Lake is 14 kilometers (approximately 8.7 miles) wide at its broadest point but plunges to a maximum depth of 310 meters (930 feet). There can be extremely high winds, not unlike an inland sea. Beautiful, privately owned chateaux, as well as vineyards, mountains, and charming villages, line the lake.

There are many outdoor cafes that serve this regional specialty, and it is absolutely delicious poached in a court bouillon, served with a tangy lemon sauce. Either fresh ocean or lake perch can be used in this recipe, or sole fillets can be substituted. This dish is typically served with thin, crisply cooked pommes frites (French fries) or steamed potatoes and a green salad with Yodeling Yogurt Dressing (page 65).

Lake Geneva Perch Filets
Serves 4

Court Bouillon
1 cup water
1/3 cup dry white wine
3 sprigs fresh dill

2 pounds perch filets

Sauce
2/3 cup cream
1 tablespoon fresh lemon juice
2 teaspoons cornstarch
1 cup reserved court bouillon
5 tablespoons chopped fresh parsley
Sea salt
Freshly ground black pepper
Fresh dill sprigs for garnish

First, make the court bouillon by placing water, white wine, and fresh dill in a large pot. Cover and bring just to a boil; turn off heat and let stand for 10 minutes. Add perch filets to pot and return to heat; simmer for approximately 5 minutes with cover on until cooked. The filets will be firm to the touch once cooked. Remove pan from heat and drain the court bouillon, reserving one cup. Place the filets on a serving dish; cover with foil to keep warm.

Meanwhile, make the sauce. Mix cream, lemon juice, and cornstarch in a small saucepan. Whisk while adding reserved court bouillon; simmer for 2 to 3 minutes, until slightly thickened. Add parsley, salt, and pepper. Spoon sauce over fish. Garnish with fresh dill. Serve immediately.

Outdoor lunch in the French Alps

I was first introduced to this easy dish while on a 3-week vacation on the tropical island called Pulau Langkawi, Malaysia. At that time, in 1994, this was a relatively unknown destination, filled with secluded, white sandy beaches and surrounded by the emerald-colored waters. According to fabulous myths and legends, the islands thrive with ogres and gigantic birds, warriors and fairy princesses, and battles and romance. All I can say is that one night while dining out, we left our outdoor light on, and when we returned, there were giant jungle bugs flying all over the place. The maintenance crew, and not warriors, battled them so we could get into our suite.

During the day, we rented motorcycles to travel around the lush terrain and loved eating at out-of-the-way beaches during our explorations. We always found little bamboo and palm branch shacks serving as restaurants, with spider monkeys swinging from the palms nearby. Communicating in sign language with the cook, we managed to choose fresh luncheon treats from the tiny menu. Once served, we sat on benches under huge palms for shade and watched the monkeys. A healthy plate filled with goodness would be served to us to savor every bite. And life just seemed to be . . . To add to this simple pleasure, everything was as Cayce recommended—locally grown and seasonal.

If you have access to an Asian market, buy lemongrass to use as skewers. If you cannot find these, then use normal bamboo or metal ones found in your supermarket. Not everyone loves lemongrass, but I find the fragrance it emits to be sweet and rather exotic. Serve with brown rice and Asian Slaw (page 51), if desired.

Asian Shrimp Skewers and Peanut Sauce
Serves 4

Sauce
1/8 cup Asian fish sauce
1/8 cup fresh lime juice
1/8 cup pineapple juice
1/8 cup soy sauce
1/8 cup rice wine vinegar
1 teaspoon finely minced, peeled fresh ginger
1 tablespoon chopped fresh cilantro

To make the sauce, stir ingredients together in a medium bowl. Set aside.

1 pound jumbo (16 to 20 per pound) shrimp, peeled, with tails left intact, deveined
1 tablespoon vegetable oil
1/2 teaspoon freshly ground black pepper
2 limes, quartered
8 lemongrass stalks, soaked in water 20 minutes

Steamed rice
Fresh cilantro sprigs for garnish

Prepare grill for cooking. (Preheat gas grill to medium high with hood closed. Light and heat until medium high.)

In a large bowl, combine shrimp with oil and pepper. Thread shrimp and fresh limes onto skewers. Grill shrimp, turning once, until cooked through—they will lose their pink color and turn red.

Serve on a platter of rice garnished with fresh cilantro sprigs, and accompany with sauce.

In the Mediterranean countries, fish is prepared in countless ways. This is a pleasing recipe that is best-suited for grilling, but the kabobs can also be cooked under the broiler or grilled on the stove top in a ridged, cast-iron skillet. If you have ever traveled to Greece or Turkey, you will have seen these yummy delights in many restaurants.

The key to great cuisine is simplicity. By utilizing fresh herbs, good quality olive oil, and fresh lemons, you have a tasty meal.

Serve this dish with freshly grilled asparagus, steamed carrots, and organic brown rice for an appealing platter.

You will need lemongrass or metal skewers for this recipe

Mediterranean Fish Kabobs
Serves 4

Marinade
4 tablespoons extra virgin olive oil
3 tablespoons freshly squeezed lemon or lime juice
1 garlic clove, crushed (optional)
Sea salt
Cracked black pepper
1 tablespoon chopped fresh thyme

1 1/2 pounds tuna or ahi, cut into 1-inch cubes
2 small red onions, quartered
2 red peppers, quartered
2 lemons, cut in half, then quartered
Fresh thyme sprigs and fresh lemon wedges for garnish

Prepare outdoor grill, if using, or have ready a ridged, cast-iron skillet on stove top.

To prepare the marinade, whisk together olive oil, lemon juice, garlic, salt, pepper, and thyme in a medium mixing bowl. Add cubed pieces of fish; let marinate in refrigerator for no longer than 30 minutes.

Thread the fish onto lemongrass skewers or lightly oiled, flat, metal skewers, alternating with onions, red peppers, and lemon wedges. Lightly brush the grill or ridged skillet with oil to prevent sticking. Add kabobs and cook for approximately 6 to 8 minutes, depending on desired doneness. Remove kabobs from skewers; place on a large serving platter over brown rice. Top the periphery of the platter with steamed vegetables. Garnish with fresh thyme and lemon.

Flounder is a strange-looking, flat creature with both eyes on one side of its head. It has a very fine, tender yet firm texture. The taste is quite delicate and sweet, and the fish is very low in fat. Flounder should not be overcooked. It is easy to tell when it is done: the flesh will turn white. Flounder is best oven-baked or sautéed lightly on the stove top. It is not a fish that can be grilled.

I tried making this one evening using my daughter Brooke's low-fat pesto sauce, substituting water for olive oil, so as not to overpower the delicate taste of the flounder. This is the delicious variation that was produced. Wild rice and steamed vegetables are a healthy accompaniment to this.

Flounder with Pesto Sauce
Serves 4

Low-Fat Pesto Sauce
1 large bunch basil
2 cloves garlic
1 cup toasted pine nuts
1/4 cup water

2 pounds flounder

Preheat oven to 350°. Line a large baking dish with unbleached parchment paper. To make pesto, place the basil, garlic, and toasted pine nuts in your food processor; process mixture until a thick paste forms. If it is too dry, add more water.

Place flounder on prepared baking sheet; baste both sides of fish with pesto sauce. Pop fish into the oven and bake for approximately 15 minutes. Serve immediately.

I have replicated a dish I often order as an appetizer in a local seafood restaurant. Their concoction uses tiny shrimp, but I prefer jumbo ones and lump crabmeat as the filler. I have also used sea scallops, which are sweet and tender and in abundance in this area. Sour cream and tomato salsa accompany these yummy delights. Sliced avocado is also a tasty and nutritious accompaniment. This is an original and innovative way to introduce seafood to young children.

Seafood Quesadillas
Serves 4

1 tablespoon sunflower oil
2 cloves garlic, minced
1/4 cup minced red onion
1 medium tomato, diced
8 medium-size whole wheat tortillas
1 pound cooked shrimp
1 pound lump crab meat
1 pound grilled scallops
1 cup grated cheddar cheese

Tomato Sauce
Heat sunflower oil in a small sauté pan. Add garlic and onion; cook over medium-high heat for approximately 3 minutes, until soft. Add diced tomatoes and cook for 2 minutes.

To assemble, place 4 tortillas on work surface. Top with shrimp, crab, scallops, prepared tomato sauce, and cheddar. Place remaining tortillas on top of this mixture.

In an ungreased large skillet, cook assembled tortillas one at a time over medium-high heat for 3 minutes on each side, being careful not to break. Alternatively, use a panini grill.

Serve with sour cream, salsa, and avocado slices.

My daughter Bree and I love this dish, and this is her recipe. This noodle-based meal can be put together in very little time, but it looks like it took hours. It is delicious with or without the shrimp. A wok is indispensable to use, as a frying pan has a larger surface and the ingredients will cook too quickly. Woks can be purchased at a relatively inexpensive price at Asian markets.

The harmony of flavors in this dish is perfect for a romantic dinner for two or for a large buffet-style dinner. You can replace the shrimp with chicken or, if vegan, leave both out and add firm tofu!

Shrimp Pad Thai
Serves 4

4 cups boiling water
1 pound Pad Thai rice noodles
1 tablespoon sunflower oil
3 cloves garlic, minced
4 *eggs*
2 medium-size *tomatoes* (about 1 pound), diced
20 large shrimp, shelled and deveined
1 tablespoon beet sugar
2 tablespoons low-sodium soy sauce
1 tablespoon Pad Thai sauce
2 tablespoons lime juice
1/4 pound crunchy bean sprouts
6 spring onions, including greens tips, chopped
1 cup crushed peanuts
1 jalapeño pepper, seeded and chopped
Lime wedges for garnish
Cilantro sprigs for garnish

Place 4 cups boiling water in a large bowl. Add noodles and let sit until soft, approximately 3 minutes; drain.

Meanwhile, heat a large wok over medium-high heat. Add oil and garlic; cook for 1 minute. Add eggs and scramble well, stirring often. Put eggs to the side of the wok; add tomatoes and shrimp; stir. Reduce heat to medium; add sugar, soy sauce, Pad Thai sauce, and lime juice; stir.

Once the shrimp is cooked, add drained Pad Thai noodles; mix all together while cooking. Add more soy sauce or Pad Thai sauce, if desired; mix well. Add fresh bean sprouts, spring onions, half the crushed peanuts, and jalapeño; mix well. Garnish with lime wedges, fresh cilantro, and remaining crushed peanuts. Have additional Pad Thai and soy sauces on the table should people wish to have more.

Variation: If making a vegan dish, replace chicken/shrimp with garden peas and sugar snap peas.

In French restaurants this creamy sauce will normally be served over a thick steak. However, I happen to find it equally splendid on white fish. It is not something you will find often, so if you want to impress someone special, this might cast the magical spell. Once you get into the hang of making sauces, you will realize how basic they are and what depth they add to simple food.

The French are adept at making sauces. At one point, my body was accustomed to eating them often. However, I now prefer simple seasonings. But this is fun for a once-in-a-while treat!

We are so blessed to have an abundance of rockfish or striped sea bass in southern Virginia. Recently I went to a dock nearby where fishing boats come in with their fresh catch of the day. I like to buy directly from fishermen if I can. So I came home with a 14-pound rockfish that had just been caught in the ocean. Now that is a supreme example of buying and eating local, in-season food.

I would suggest serving this delight with parsley rice to sop up the sauce. Steamed carrots and yellow squash are a nice accompaniment as well. The more color in your diet, the better your health will be.

White Fish with Mushroom Sauce
Serves 4

2-pound white fish filet (rockfish, halibut, or bass)
1 tablespoon extra virgin olive oil

Sauce
1 tablespoon *butter*
1 clove garlic, minced
1 tablespoon grain mustard
1 cup heavy *cream*
2 tablespoons brandy
1/2 cup chopped button mushrooms
Cracked black pepper

Preheat oven to 400°. Line baking sheet with unbleached parchment paper. Thoroughly wash fish filet; pat dry. Place fish on prepared baking sheet; brush lightly with olive oil. Bake for 20 minutes, turning once after 10 minutes.

Meanwhile, make the sauce. Heat butter in a medium-size saucepan. Add garlic; cook and stir until garlic is tender. Do not brown. Add grain mustard; cook, stirring constantly, while adding heavy cream, brandy, and mushrooms, until sauce is thickened. Season with pepper.

Transfer cooked fish to a serving platter. Pour sauce over fish. Serve immediately.

Salmon cakes are usually made with leftover mashed potatoes to make for a tasty meal. I prefer to use sweet potatoes. This is a relatively inexpensive meal and a great one for children. I have used Asian-inspired spices and herbs in this, but they can be replaced by fresh parsley and chopped spring onions. Salmon cakes are great for a casual weeknight dinner. Serve with a salad of your choice.

Asian Salmon Cakes
Serves 4

2 cans (8-ounce) salmon, drained
2 cups mashed sweet *potatoes*
2 tablespoons diced spring onions
2 *eggs*
1 teaspoon low-sodium soy sauce
1 teaspoon ground ginger
1/4 teaspoon white pepper
1 teaspoon sunflower oil
Fresh parsley for garnish

Mix salmon, sweet potatoes, spring onions, eggs, soy sauce, ginger, and pepper in a large bowl. Shape into 4 round patties. Melt oil in a large skillet. Turn heat to medium high and place patties in skillet. Cook for approximately 4 minutes, or until golden brown. Flip patties over and cook for another 4 minutes. Garnish with fresh parsley. Serve immediately.

The first time I visited the rugged coasts of Brittany and Normandy, I had the pleasure of eating fresh mussels often and in many different ways. Mussels are rich yet fragrant when paired with shallots, garlic, and wine. This dish is elegant as a first course or served as a meal with toasted bread to soak up the aromatic broth. This is my favorite version, for its simplicity and because I happen to love garlic!

Steamed Mussels in Wine
Serves 4

2 tablespoons *butter*
2 shallots, minced
2 cloves garlic, minced
4 pounds mussels, scrubbed and debearded
1 cup dry white wine
1/4 cup minced parsley
1/4 teaspoon white pepper

Melt butter in a large stockpot on medium heat. Add shallots and garlic and cook for 3 minutes. Do not brown. Add mussels and wine; cover. Allow to steam for approximately 5 minutes. The mussels should open at this point. Discard any that have not opened. Remove mussels from pot with a slotted spoon and place in a large serving bowl.

Cook remaining broth over medium-high heat until it is reduced to one cup. Add parsley and pepper. Place mussels in large soup bowls and pour broth over them. Serve immediately.

Variation: Incorporate 1/4 cup heavy cream just before serving.

Of Fowl and Lamb

Living in Saudi Arabia for four years and traveling often in the Middle East opened up my taste buds to the many wonderful spices used and the various ways to prepare lamb. One night, I had the pleasure of driving to a friend's horse stables in the desert surrounding Jeddah. It was a full moon, so we could see clearly. Feisty Arabian stallions were saddled for us and off we went. Actually, I decided to gallop, not knowing that the other horses would follow suit. Not everyone was adept at galloping through the desert, so I got into a bit of hot water and felt so guilty. All was forgotten once we returned to the stables. I could not believe my eyes. There were beautiful Persian carpets laid over the sand for us to dine on under the stars. Deliciously roasted lamb was served to us with heaping bowls of steamed rice and vegetables. It is one of those moments that leave a lifelong memory.

In this chapter, I have tried to include unusual yet easy-to-make meat dishes for you from around the world. By just using varied herbs and spices, you can make the simplest cut of chicken or lamb taste like a celebratory dinner. And it's nice to try a new take on familiar foods. For example, instead of consuming burgers made with beef, why not try Asian turkey burgers or Middle Eastern lamb burgers? These are much healthier options—lower in fat and easier to digest. Cayce and many health experts suggest that eating red meat be kept to a minimum. A great roast chicken or duck or quail is lower in fat and a great source of protein. And eating wild game when in season may give us nutrients not found in their domesticated counterparts, according to the Cayce readings.

Kids seem to love eating chicken, and I have included some unusual family recipes in this section to add a bit of spice to the same old chicken fingers. Variety should be a part of a child's diet so that they do not develop that nasty habit of being picky eaters. Their taste buds should be exposed to many new flavors at an early age, and as the old adage reminds us, There's no time like the present. Leftover roast chicken or turkey to make them healthy snacks or sandwiches is a great alternative to using nitrate-filled deli meats.

It is very important to feed your family free-range and organically raised poultry and grass-fed lamb. The flesh is leaner, as the animals are actually outside exercising and feeding from fields of grass. Utopia! Nothing makes me happier than the sight of a local farm with animals roaming freely and grazing, as they should. Yes, it is more expensive, but the health benefits far outweigh the costs. By choosing organic meat, you are avoiding the consumption of GMOs (genetically modified organisms), as this is put in the feed of conventionally raised animals. Most farmers markets now make organic and free-range poultry and lamb available.

Organic meat is sought after by cooks and chefs who are searching for quality and great taste—the taste of free-range meat is so superior, it is amazing—and concerned about the well-being of animals.

A few precautions are in order when preparing raw poultry and meats. Always thoroughly wash poultry before cooking. Also, use separate work surfaces for meat, poultry, and vegetables. Poultry cannot be eaten undercooked. When the juices run clear, it is done. But always check the thickest portion (the thigh, when cooking a whole chicken or turkey) to ensure that it is done, or use a meat thermometer to be sure. Also, thoroughly wash your hands, scrubbing well for at least 60 seconds, after handling meats.

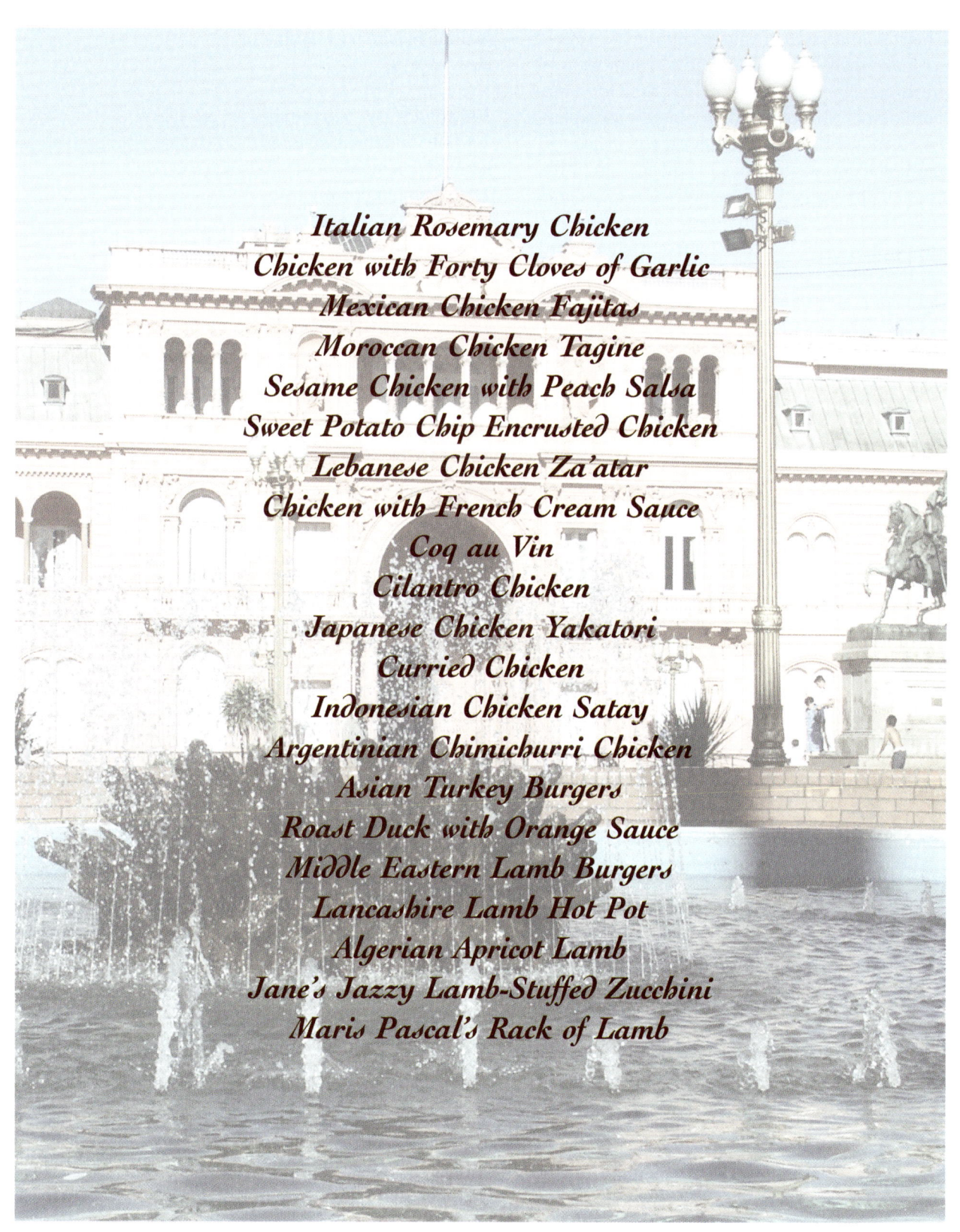

Italian Rosemary Chicken
Chicken with Forty Cloves of Garlic
Mexican Chicken Fajitas
Moroccan Chicken Tagine
Sesame Chicken with Peach Salsa
Sweet Potato Chip Encrusted Chicken
Lebanese Chicken Za'atar
Chicken with French Cream Sauce
Coq au Vin
Cilantro Chicken
Japanese Chicken Yakatori
Curried Chicken
Indonesian Chicken Satay
Argentinian Chimichurri Chicken
Asian Turkey Burgers
Roast Duck with Orange Sauce
Middle Eastern Lamb Burgers
Lancashire Lamb Hot Pot
Algerian Apricot Lamb
Jane's Jazzy Lamb-Stuffed Zucchini
Maris Pascal's Rack of Lamb

This Italian version of baking chicken is an easy-to-make dish. The combination of lemons and fresh rosemary roasted slowly makes for a superb dinner. This is definitely a family-style platter to be presented with a gorgeous display of fresh garden vegetables. Typically, in Italy, roasted potatoes accompany this. I suggest serving crisply cooked potato skins, as they are much healthier. Carrots, garden peas, and sautéed onions make for a complete meal filled with color, nutrition, and flavor.

Italian Rosemary Chicken
Serves 6-8

3-4 pounds *chicken*, trimmed of excess fat
2 whole lemons, quartered
Juice of 2 lemons
2 tablespoons lemon zest
2-3 tablespoons olive oil
1 teaspoon sea salt
1 teaspoon black pepper
3 tablespoons finely chopped fresh rosemary
Lemon slices for garnish
Rosemary sprigs for garnish

Preheat oven to 375°. Thoroughly wash and pat dry chicken; remove any excess fat. Line a roasting pan with parchment paper.

Place lemon quarters in the cavity of chicken. Rub lemon juice, lemon zest, olive oil, salt, pepper, and rosemary over whole chicken, making sure it is thoroughly coated.

Place chicken on prepared roasting pan. Bake for approximately 45 minutes. Brush chicken with pan drippings, and continue to cook for an additional 50 minutes or until skin is crispy brown and the juices run clear (breasts should have an internal temperature of 165°F).

Let rest, covered in foil, for 10 minutes before carving. Pour the juices from the pan into a serving bowl. Use a spoon to skim the fat off the top. Serve the chicken with the juices on the side or a little poured over the top of the chicken. Garnish with lemon slices and rosemary sprigs.

Even if you do not like garlic, I promise you will love this classic French delight. Although it may sound misleading, by poaching garlic in a delicious broth of wine and fresh thyme, a sweet flavor is rendered. This is a relatively easy recipe to make but very elegant served with parsley and lemon rice and accompanied with steamed French green beans.

Do not even think of throwing away the garlic once it is cooked—you can use it as a spread instead of butter, and it will melt in your mouth.

This is a dish that can be made a day in advance. Just reheat in the oven or on your stove top.

**Chicken with Forty Cloves of Garlic
(Poulet aux quarante gousses d'ail)
Serves 6**

2-3 unpeeled heads of garlic
5 tablespoons *butter*
6 *chicken* breasts, bone in and skin on
1 teaspoon dried thyme
Sea salt
Freshly ground black pepper
1 cup dry white wine
1 1/2 cups *chicken broth*
Fresh thyme for garnish

Place garlic cloves in a small pot of boiling water; blanch for 10 minutes.

Warm butter in a deep skillet; turn heat to medium high and add chicken pieces skin side down. Brown chicken breasts on both sides to seal in flavor. Place garlic and thyme around chicken pieces; season lightly with salt and pepper; cover. Cook chicken over low heat for 45 minutes, or until juices run clear (breasts should have an internal temperature of 165°F). Remove chicken pieces; place on a serving platter and cover with foil.

Discard any fat from the pan; add wine and put on high heat. Stir occasionally until liquid is reduced by half. Once liquid is reduced, add chicken broth and reduce again until you have about 1 cup.

Pour sauce over the chicken. Garnish with sprigs of fresh thyme.

When one thinks of a Mexican restaurant, this sizzling dish often comes to mind. It is usually served on a searing-hot sheet of granite, but most of us do not have that at home. A nice, heated serving platter will do fine. By letting the chicken marinate overnight, you will have a regal-tasting dinner. Do not let the list of ingredients daunt you, for they are quickly assembled. Kids seem to love this dish because it is colorful and fun to put together at the table. This is great for a family-style dinner or for entertaining a group. Grab a warm tortilla, fill it with sizzling chicken and vegetables, top it with Chunky Guacamole and sour cream, and you have one great fajita!

Mexican Chicken Fajitas
Serves 4

Marinade
1 teaspoon ground cumin
1 teaspoon garlic powder
1 teaspoon onion powder
1/2 teaspoon cayenne pepper
1 tablespoon hot chili paste
1 tablespoon maple syrup
1/4 cup olive oil
1/4 cup roughly chopped fresh cilantro
1/2 cup fresh lime juice
1/2 cup fresh orange juice
2 tablespoons orange zest

For the fajitas
2 pounds skinless, boneless chicken tenders
1 tablespoon sunflower oil
2 tablespoons olive oil
2 large red onions, cut into 1/4-inch-thick slices
1 large yellow bell pepper, cut into 1/4-inch-thick slices
1 large red bell pepper, cut into 1/4-inch-thick slices
8 tortillas, warmed before serving
Fresh cilantro sprigs for garnish
Lime wedges for garnish
Sour cream
Chunky Guacamole (page 10)

In a medium-size bowl, mix marinade ingredients well. Place chicken tenders and marinade in a gallon-size freezer bag or a non-reactive container. Refrigerate overnight or up to 24 hours.

To begin the cooking process, heat sunflower oil in a large skillet on medium-high heat. Add chicken tenders; cook approximately 10 minutes, turning once, until juices run clear (internal temperature should be 165°F). Do not overcook or chicken will become dry.

While chicken is cooking, heat olive oil in another large skillet over medium-high heat. Add onion slices; cook, stirring constantly, until slightly brown, about 3 minutes. Add red and yellow pepper slices; cook approximately 2 minutes.

Once chicken is cooked, warm the tortillas. Place chicken and vegetables on a large serving platter. Top with fresh cilantro sprigs and surround with lime wedges. Spoon sour cream and guacamole into small, separate serving bowls. Keep tortillas warm in a basket lined with a cloth napkin. Everyone help yourself!

Of Fowl and Lamb

Oh, what a glorious dish this is! with typical Moroccan spices wafting through your kitchen as your company arrives. Or your family quickly drops whatever they are doing to follow the scent of cinnamon and cumin. There are so many versions of tagine that it would take a lifetime of cooking to try them all. I have readjusted a Moroccan friend's version here, using dried apricots and dates rather than prunes.

I like to serve this dish over a bed of couscous garnished with preserved lemons or fresh lemon wedges. This recipe normally calls for a whole chicken, but it is much easier to use skinless chicken breasts.

Moroccan Chicken Tagine
Serves 4

4 pounds skinless, bone-in *chicken* breasts
1 teaspoon ground black pepper
1/2 teaspoon sea salt
3 teaspoons ground cumin
1 cup dried apricots
1 cup pitted dates
3-4 teaspoons ground cinnamon
2 large yellow onions, sliced 1/2 inch thick
1 tablespoon ground ginger
1 teaspoon turmeric
2 tablespoons sunflower oil
Sea salt
Freshly ground black pepper
Preserved lemons or lemon wedges for garnish

Thoroughly wash chicken breasts; pat dry with paper towels. Rub chicken with pepper, salt, and cumin; let stand for 30 to 60 minutes.

Meanwhile, place apricots, dates, and cinnamon in a large pot with enough water to cover. Bring just to a boil; simmer for approximately 30 minutes, stirring occasionally.

Add sliced onions, ginger, turmeric, and more water, if necessary, to pot; simmer for at least 10 minutes, until onions are soft.

Meanwhile, in a large skillet, heat oil; brown chicken breasts over medium-high heat. Once browned, add chicken to apricot and date mixture; cover. Cook over medium-low heat for approximately 30 minutes, until chicken is very tender (internal temperature should be 165°F). Taste sauce and season to taste with salt and pepper.

Plate chicken on a large serving platter. Cover with the dates, apricots, and sauce. Garnish with preserved lemons or lemon wedges.

This dish is refreshing and the sesame seeds add a nice little crunch. This is a great replacement for fried chicken, which is not recommended for a healthy diet. The marinade is inspired by Asian ingredients. Toasted sesame seeds are readily available in most grocery stores or Middle Eastern or Asian markets. Fresh peach salsa, baked sweet potatoes, and other steamed vegetables make for a colorful and healthy plate. If you have any leftovers, the chicken can be used to top a luncheon salad.

Sesame Chicken with Peach Salsa
Serves 4

Marinade
2 tablespoons low-sodium soy sauce
2 tablespoons honey
1 teaspoon grated fresh ginger
1/4 teaspoon cayenne pepper

1 pound boneless, skinless *chicken* tenders

Peach Salsa
2 ripe but firm *peaches*, cut into 1/2-inch dice
1/2 red onion, diced
1/2 *yellow pepper*, seeded and diced
1 small jalapeño pepper, seeded and diced
1 tablespoon fresh lime juice
1 tablespoon olive oil
1/4 cup chopped fresh cilantro

1 cup toasted sesame seeds
1 tablespoon sunflower oil

In a medium-size bowl, mix marinade ingredients well. Place chicken tenders and marinade in a gallon-size freezer bag or a non-reactive container. Refrigerate for 2 to 3 hours.

Meanwhile, prepare the peach salsa. Place prepared peaches, onions, pepper, and jalapeño in a medium-size bowl. In a small bowl, whisk together lime juice, olive oil, and fresh cilantro. Pour over peach mixture; cover and refrigerate.

Remove chicken tenders from marinade and wipe them dry. Reserve 1 cup of marinade. Roll chicken pieces in toasted sesame seeds. In a medium-size skillet, melt sunflower oil over medium-high heat. Add chicken; cook for 5 minutes. Remove chicken and place in a large, ovenproof casserole. Finish cooking in a 150°F oven for 10 to 15 minutes, or until juices run clear (internal temperature should be 165°F).

Pour reserved marinade into small saucepan; heat over medium heat while chicken is cooking. Reduce by half. Place chicken pieces on serving dish. Serve with sauce.

This is my mum's recipe and something she served to me as a child. Even though I lived in the South for the first nine years of my life, I do not remember ever eating anything fried. This was about as close as we got to that, I guess. I used to love it when she would make this for any friends staying over for a sleepover. I knew how much they loved it. I think drumsticks are particularly great for this, as kids and not so little kids can just pick them up with their hands and chomp away. A simple salad served with Ranch dressing and some steamed veggies would be an ideal and healthy accompaniment. You do not want to have two starches in one meal, so forget the potatoes, as in French fries.

**Sweet Potato Chip Encrusted Chicken
Serves 4**

8 *chicken* drumsticks, skin on
2 tablespoons fresh lemon juice
1 cup crushed organic sweet potato chips

Preheat oven to 400°. Line a baking sheet with unbleached parchment paper.

Thoroughly wash drumsticks; pat dry with paper towels. Squeeze lemon juice evenly over chicken. Place crushed potato chips in a medium-size bowl. Roll chicken in the chips to cover them evenly. Place chicken on prepared baking sheet, and bake for approximately 35 minutes, or until juices run clear (internal temperature should be 165°F).

This is a superlative dish from Lebanon. It is their version of fried chicken. It would be my choice any day of the week and is another easy and versatile recipe that will delight your family and friends. The longer you marinate the chicken, the tastier it will be. This can be done hours or even one to two days ahead.

I am partial to za'atar (the traditional Arabic blend of local herbs from the mint family) and have found that once people try it, they absolutely crave it. In Lebanon there is a belief that this particular herbal blend makes the mind alert and keeps the body strong. For this reason, children are encouraged to eat a za'atar sandwich for breakfast before an exam. Once again, you can easily find this herb mixture in Middle Eastern markets, or it can be ordered online. Or if you would like to make your own, it's very simple (see Za'atar, page xx).

I serve this chicken with raita (page 7) and Fatima's Fatoush Salad (page 38). You are going to absolutely love this one, and it will be a keeper, for sure.

Lebanese Chicken Za'atar
Serves 4

4 pieces skin-on, bone-in chicken breasts (about 2 pounds)
1/4 cup olive oil
8 tablespoons za'atar

Place chicken, oil, and za'atar in a gallon-size freezer bag or a non-reactive container; refrigerate for a couple of hours or up to 2 days.

Preheat oven to 425°. Line a large baking sheet with unbleached parchment paper. Place chicken pieces skin side up on baking sheet. Make sure you put all the marinade on top of chicken. Bake for approximately 45 minutes, until crispy tender.

This is another easy recipe that is often served in Swiss or French homes. It takes no time at all, and the taste is in the creamy sauce with mustard and garlic. This is also a great dish to serve at a dinner party because it is so versatile. (If you do not have Herbes de Provence on hand, use 1 teaspoon of dried thyme or basil.) Normally, this is served with steamed rice, steamed veggies, and a green salad with a vinaigrette of your choice.

Chicken with French Cream Sauce
Serves 4

1 tablespoon *butter*
1 pound *chicken* tenders
2 cloves garlic, minced
1 tablespoon Dijon mustard
1 teaspoon Herbes de Provence
Sea salt
1 cup heavy *cream*

Melt butter in a medium skillet; add chicken tenders and brown over medium heat. Remove chicken from pan. Add garlic; cook and stir for 3 minutes. Do not let garlic brown. Add Dijon mustard, Herbes de Provence, and salt; gradually stir in cream until all ingredients are incorporated. Add chicken tenders and let simmer over low heat for 15 minutes.

This is another great French way of cooking chicken. It used to be quite common to find this dish in restaurants, but it is seldom seen on menus anymore. So I thought it would be a nice surprise to include this yummy, wine-based dinner. This is definitely for a dinner party, and anyone who tastes it will agree that it is flavor-intensive.

The original version of this recipe calls for a whole chicken, cut in pieces. If you prefer, and if it is easier for you, buy chicken breasts. The taste will be the same! Pearl onions can be found peeled and frozen now. I highly recommend using these, unless you have the patience of Job to peel these little onions. Serving this with wild rice and a composed salad (use a hearty lettuce, such as romaine) would be delicious.

Coq au Vin
Serves 6

4 pounds bone-in, skin-on *chicken* breasts
Sea salt
Freshly ground black pepper
2 tablespoons olive oil
2 tablespoon *butter*
1 pound pearl onions, peeled
1 pound button mushrooms, sliced 1/2-inch thick
2 tablespoons flour
3-4 cups dry red wine
1 cup *chicken* stock
2 tablespoons Herbes de Provence

Preheat oven to 325°. Thoroughly wash the chicken pieces; pat dry. Season chicken with salt and pepper. Heat oil in a heavy skillet; add chicken to skillet skin side down; brown on both sides over medium-high heat.

Meanwhile, in a large, enamel casserole dish, heat butter over medium heat. Add onions; cook and stir until browned. Add mushrooms; cook and stir until golden brown. Sprinkle flour on top and stir; cook for 2 minutes. Add wine and stock; whisk until no lumps remain; bring to a boil. Add chicken pieces and herbs; lower heat to simmer. Cover casserole and bake in oven for one hour, or until juices run clear from the thickest part of meat (internal temperature should be 165°F).

Of Fowl and Lamb

This is a delicious way to make chicken come alive. My daughter Bree is a vegetarian but often puts her tastes aside to create meat dishes for her partner, Luc, and her daughter, Anais. I would suggest allowing the chicken to marinate overnight, but it's also great when made spur of the moment. By incorporating fresh herbs in your cooking, it is surprising how out of the ordinary dishes become. Bree serves this dish with steamed rice and vegetables.

Cilantro Chicken
Serves 2

2 tablespoons low-sodium soy sauce
4 tablespoons olive oil
2 tablespoons beet sugar
2 tablespoons grain mustard
1/2 cup chopped cilantro
2 cloves garlic, minced
1 pound boneless, skinless *chicken* breasts

In a large bowl, whisk together soy sauce, olive oil, beet sugar, mustard, cilantro, and garlic. Place marinade in a large freezer bag and add chicken breasts. Store chicken and marinade in refrigerator until ready to use.

Preheat oven to 350°. Place chicken and marinade in an ovenproof casserole. Bake for 30 to 40 minutes, until golden brown.

Bree, Luc, Anais and Sienna at an outdoor restaurant at Lake Geneva

Living in Geneva for twenty-two years was truly an international and cosmopolitan experience. Almost every agency of the United Nations and Red Cross is represented there. For a time, I worked for U.N.H.C.R. (United Nations High Commissioner for Refugees), where I had the opportunity to meet people from all over the globe. Although I did not know many Japanese nationals, I was introduced to their traditional cuisine at a dinner party. This is probably one of their most popular dishes, and I think you will enjoy it too. This dish is typically served with rice, stir-fried vegetables, and a green salad with Asian vinaigrette (see Ah-So Asian Dressing, page 68).

Japanese Chicken Yakatori
Serves 4

2 pounds boneless, skinless *chicken* breasts, cut into bite-size cubes

Marinade
2 tablespoons shoyu (Japanese soy sauce)
2 tablespoons sake
2 tablespoons beet sugar
3 cloves garlic, skinned and crushed
2-inch piece of fresh ginger, peeled and crushed
Freshly ground black pepper

Sauce
2 tablespoons shoyu
2 tablespoons sake
2 tablespoons beet sugar
Freshly ground black pepper

To make the marinade, place shoyu, sake, sugar, garlic, ginger, and black pepper in a small bowl. Whisk well until the sugar has dissolved. Place chicken and marinade in a gallon-size freezer bag or non-reactive bowl with cover; refrigerate for at least 4 hours or up to 3 days.

When ready to cook, remove chicken from marinade and thread onto metal skewers. Grill over medium-high heat on outdoor barbeque or under a broiler for 10-15 minutes, turning the skewers frequently and brushing with the marinade.

While the chicken is cooking, make the sauce. Place shoyu, sake, and sugar in a small saucepan; season to taste with pepper; simmer for several minutes. Serve the yakatori hot, with the sauce poured over it.

Of Fowl and Lamb

My mother made this all the time for dinner parties when I was young. I have never met a curry I did not like. I have made curries from scratch, but it is labor intensive and I don't think most people wish to take the time to do that. So the alternative is buying a good quality curry paste, which is available in the exotic food section of your grocery store or in an Asian/Indian market.

This curry is made great with all the little side dishes that accompany it.

Curried Chicken
Serves 4

2 tablespoons grape seed oil
2 medium-size yellow onions, diced
2 cloves garlic, minced
2 tablespoons medium-hot curry paste
1 teaspoon ground coriander
3 tablespoons *tomato paste*
1 (8-ounce) can coconut milk
2 pounds boneless, skinless *chicken*, cut into 1-inch pieces
1/4 cup *chicken* stock

Accompaniments
2 bananas, peeled and chopped
1 medium-size yellow onion, diced
1 cup cashew nuts
3 hard-boiled *eggs*, peeled and diced
1 cup unsulphured raisins
Mango chutney
1 cup raita (page 7)

Pour oil into a large pot. Add onions and garlic; cook over medium heat for 3 to 4 minutes, until soft. Add curry paste, coriander, and tomato paste; stir until well mixed. Add coconut milk; stir. Add chicken pieces and stock; cover. Cook for approximately 15 minutes, stirring once. Serve with steamed rice and accompaniments.

I had a wonderful opportunity to travel to Bali in 1978, before tourists invaded this idyllic island. At that time, only propeller planes could fly onto the tiny runway. The curtains that separated the pilot from the passengers were opened for us to see the sudden approach over the Straits of Bali. It was quite an experience in how to keep your cool under extreme duress.

Bali is an enchanting island, and I immediately fell in love with the people, the culture, and the food. While journeying up a mountain on a motorcycle one day, we came across a roadside satay stand. It was my first experience with this delicious way of eating chicken, which is served with a wonderfully soothing peanut sauce. I have ordered satay in many restaurants and have been disappointed. This recipe from my eldest niece and incredible hostess, Tiffany Mackay Donohue, is the real deal and as close as it gets to Indonesian satay. This is wonderful to serve at a dinner party with steamed rice and a green salad. Alternatively, this is equally superb served as an hors d'oeuvre. You will never order this in a restaurant again after making this!

Indonesian Chicken Satay
Serves 4

Marinade
1 teaspoon pepper
1 teaspoon ground cumin
1 teaspoon ground coriander
1/2 teaspoon turmeric
1 teaspoon minced garlic
1 tablespoon honey
1 tablespoon vegetable oil
1 tablespoon low-sodium soy sauce
1 tablespoon lemon juice
1 tablespoon fish sauce

1 pound skinless, boneless chicken breasts, cut into cubes or thin slices

Peanut Sauce
1/2 cup crunchy peanut butter
2 tablespoons low-sodium soy sauce
3 cloves garlic, minced
1/2 cup hot water
1/4 cup chopped cilantro
3 tablespoons red wine vinegar
2 tablespoons honey
3/4 teaspoon dried crushed red pepper flakes
Fresh cilantro and lime wedges for garnish

In a large mixing bowl, add all marinade ingredients and stir to combine. Pour into a gallon-size zip-lock bag. Add chicken pieces and seal. Refrigerate for at least 4 hours or overnight and up to 2 days.

Meanwhile, to make peanut sauce, place ingredients in a medium saucepan over medium heat. Stir and cook until ingredients form a smooth paste. If sauce is too thick, add a bit more water.

Discard marinade; place chicken on metal skewers or well-soaked bamboo skewers. Grill over medium-high heat on outdoor barbeque or under a broiler, turning once, until golden brown. Place on serving tray. Garnish with chopped, fresh cilantro and lime wedges. Serve with hot peanut sauce.

Of Fowl and Lamb

The first time I tried this sauce, I thought I was in heaven! While working in Geneva, I had a great colleague and friend from Argentina, Alexandro. Just before he was to return to Buenos Aires with his family, we went to a beautiful park in the woods where we had a farewell barbeque. The Swiss love to picnic! Anyway, we all had to bring a dish. Alexandro brought Argentinian beef and chicken marinated in this sauce and then grilled it over hot charcoals. It was just outstanding and this is his recipe.

My good friend Charlene begs me to make this any time she comes for dinner. The sauce is what makes this dish. The longer you allow the chicken to marinade, the better it will taste. I highly recommend using freshly squeezed lemon juice, as the flavor is truly superior.

Argentinian Chimichurri Chicken
Serves 6

Chimichurri Sauce
2 bunches curly parsley, stemmed
10 cloves garlic
1 1/2 cups Spanish olive oil
6 tablespoons freshly squeezed lemon juice
2 teaspoons red pepper flakes
1 teaspoon sea salt

3 pounds skinless, boneless chicken breasts

To make the sauce, place all ingredients in a food processor and mix until you have a thick paste. Correct the seasonings with lemon juice or salt to your liking.

Place 1 cup of sauce and chicken pieces in a gallon-size zip-lock bag or non-reactive bowl with cover. Refrigerate for at least 4 hours or up to 2 days. Refrigerate remaining sauce to be served once chicken is cooked.

Preheat oven to 350°. Line baking sheet with unbleached parchment paper. Place chicken on sheet and baste with marinade. Bake for approximately 40 minutes, until crispy tender and the juices run clear (internal temperature should be 165°F).

Meanwhile, heat remaining chimichurri sauce in a small saucepan over low heat for approximately 10 minutes. Place chicken pieces with pan juices on serving platter. Serve with sauce.

Turkey is loved by many, as it is another low-fat source of protein and an ideal substitute for beef. I prefer the dark meat myself, as it is richer in flavor and more moist than the white meat. This recipe uses Asian spices to give a unique flavor. Top your burgers with Asian Slaw (page 51) instead of lettuce and tomatoes for even more great flavor. With all the intense flavors of the spices, no condiments will be necessary. Use whole wheat buns for their added fiber. Toasted buns add a tasty texture and ensure that the buns will not become too moist once the burgers are added.

Asian Turkey Burgers
Serves 4

1 pound ground *turkey meat*
1 *egg*
2 tablespoon chopped cilantro or flat-leaf parsley
1/2 teaspoon ground coriander
4 shallots, finely chopped
1 teaspoon low-sodium soy sauce
1 tablespoon *tomato puree*
1 cup toasted sesame seeds
4 whole wheat burger buns

Place ground turkey, egg, cilantro or parsley, coriander, shallots, soy sauce, and tomato puree in a medium bowl; mix well. Place toasted sesame seeds on a large plate. Make 4 turkey patties and dip in sesame seeds to completely cover.

If using outdoor grill, preheat to medium high. Grill burgers on stove-top griddle or outdoor grill until thoroughly cooked (internal temperature should be 165°F). Place burgers on buns and top with Asian slaw.

Of Fowl and Lamb

This is my grandmother's recipe for this delightful dish. Her name was Elsa and she was born on the very tiny and rugged Brier Island in Nova Scotia. This is situated on the world renowned Bay of Fundy and is worth the visit for whale watchers and people seeking total peace. You can only get there by ferry or small plane.

Nanny was a wonderful, classic cook, and by watching her, I learned many techniques. Whenever Nanny cooked duck, I was not too far off, waiting for it to come out of the oven. You could smell it from outside her cottage.

Although duck is not something most people think of cooking for dinner, when prepared well, it is a superb protein. Duck is all dark meat and quite rich. It is a nice alternative to roast chicken. There are many versions of cooking this, but I am using my nanny's, which is to cook the duck slowly and baste frequently with orange sauce. She served this with wild rice and always a nice assortment of colorful vegetables. Carrots are a wonderful choice and any others you wish.

I would highly recommend using organic duck, as the commercial ones are full of fat. And duck does tend to shrink quite a bit, as there is a lot of fat. Try to remove as much fat from the duck as you can before cooking.

Roast Duck with Orange Sauce
Serves 6

Orange Sauce
2/3 cup beet sugar
2 tablespoons cornstarch
3 tablespoons grated orange zest
1 cup fresh orange juice
4 tablespoons orange liquor (optional)

3-4 pound whole duck
1 large orange, quartered
Fresh flat-leaf parsley for garnish

Duck Gravy
Reserved drippings
1/4 cup flour
Sea salt
Freshly ground black pepper

Preheat oven to 300°. To make the sauce, combine sugar, cornstarch, orange zest, orange juice, and orange liquor, if using, in a medium saucepan. Bring to a boil; simmer for 4 to 5 minutes.

Trim duck of excess fat. Wash thoroughly and pat dry. Place 4 orange quarters in cavity of duck. Tress legs with cooking twine. Place duck in roasting pan, skin side up. Pour orange sauce on top of duck.

Bake duck for 3 hours, until the skin is crispy brown. Baste the duck with the sauce and drippings every 30 minutes. Remove drippings 30 minutes before duck is finished baking, leaving a small amount to cover the bottom of the pan. Pour drippings into a bowl and set aside. Continue to bake duck 30 more minutes. Remove duck from roasting pan and let sit for several minutes while making the gravy.

To make gravy, skim fat off the surface of reserved drippings and discard. Place the roasting pan over medium heat and whisk in 1/4 cup flour. Cook for several minutes, until flour turns golden brown. Slowly add drippings, whisking constantly until gravy thickens. Season with salt and pepper.

Carve duck as you would a whole chicken. Garnish with julienned orange peel and fresh parsley. Serve gravy in a gravy bowl.

Yummy! While filming cooking videos in Denver with my dear friends Nancy and Dennis Chrisbaum, this is one of the recipes that was highlighted. We wanted to use locally grown products, and Colorado happens to have wonderful grass-fed lamb. The film crew could not wait until it was a wrap to sit down and eat these lamb burgers. Most of the people had never tasted lamb burgers but soon became as excited about them as my family is!

For meat eaters, lamb burgers are the perfect replacement for hamburgers. This recipe is full of spice and all things nice. It is refreshing served with raita, tomatoes, lettuce, and whole wheat buns. Grilling is the best way to cook them, but a skillet will do just fine too. Lamb can be cooked medium to well done, according to your taste. These are my favorite burgers in the world!

Middle Eastern Lamb Burgers
Serves 4

1 pound grass-fed ground *lamb*
1/2 red onion, finely diced
1 1/2 teaspoons ground cumin
2 cloves garlic, minced
1/2 teaspoon cinnamon
3 tablespoons chopped fresh mint
1-2 tablespoons chopped fresh cilantro
Sea salt
Freshly ground black pepper

4 whole wheat pita pockets
4 large leaves of *red leaf* or *green leaf lettuce*
2 medium *tomatoes*, sliced
1 cup raita (page 7)

Mix lamb, onion, cumin, garlic, cinnamon, mint, cilantro, salt, and pepper in a large bowl. Form into 4 patties.

Preheat grill to medium high. If you are sautéing burgers, add 1 tablespoon of olive oil to a large skillet. Allow oil to heat on medium high. Place burgers in pan and cook for 3-4 minutes on each side. Use meat thermometer to determine desired doneness. Remove from grill or skillet.

Open pita pockets; gently place burgers in middle. Top with lettuce, tomatoes, and raita. Serve immediately.

Filming in Denver, Colorado

Of Fowl and Lamb

This recipe is from my dear friend Pauline, who is actually from Liverpool, England. After all these years of living in America, she still eats English fare. This dish is inexpensive and relatively painless to make. And it is real comfort food at its best, but healthy, to say the least. Pauline uses white potatoes but I have replaced them with sweet potatoes in this recipe, which add great color. Try serving this with some English garden peas or steamed carrots. English pickled onions are a must for the English, and they can be found in specialty markets. They really add a splendid touch to this meal. Enjoy!

Lancashire Lamb Hot Pot
Serves 4

4 (1/4-pound) lamb blades
2 large yellow onions, sliced 1/2 inch thick
4 medium-size sweet potatoes, sliced 1/2 inch thick
1-2 cups vegetable stock or water
Sea salt
Freshly ground black pepper

Preheat oven to 300°. Place lamb blades in the bottom of an ovenproof casserole. Cover with a layer of onions, then a layer of sweet potatoes. Season with sea salt and ground black pepper. Add another layer of onions followed by a layer of sweet potatoes. Add vegetable stock until it comes halfway above the first layer of lamb, onions, and potatoes. Cover casserole and cook in the oven for 4 to 5 hours.

During the last 15 minutes of cooking, remove as much extra liquid as possible and discard. Serve immediately.

Traditional Algerian food is very similar to Moroccan cuisine and shows the historic influences of Berber, Turkish, and French tastes. Although I have never been to Algeria, I do have friends from there. This is a good example of how just a few ingredients can add pizazz to a lean cube of lamb! The sweetness of the apricot is balanced by the robust taste of fresh ginger. This would typically be served with couscous or steamed rice and a fresh garden salad.

Algerian Apricot Lamb
Serves 4

1 tablespoon vegetable oil
1 large onion, sliced into 1/4-inch slivers
1 pound lean *lamb*, cubed
1 1/2 cups dried unsulphured apricots
1/4 cup apricot nectar
2-inch piece fresh ginger, peeled and grated

Heat oil in a medium skillet over medium-high heat. Add onions and lamb; cook and stir for 2-3 minutes, until lamb is browned. Add remaining ingredients; reduce heat to low. Cover and simmer gently for 40 minutes, or until lamb is tender. Serve immediately.

After a visit to our local farmers market last autumn, I came home with huge stuffing zucchini and suggested to my friend Jane that we create a new recipe for zucchini using the beautiful produce we had purchased. As I cooked, Jane documented the details and ingredients involved. It came out really well, and this is a meal in itself! The marinara sauce can be made days in advance and stored in a glasstop jar in the refrigerator.

Jane's Jazzy Lamb-Stuffed Zucchini
Serves 4

Marinara Sauce
4-5 tablespoons extra virgin olive oil
1 jalapeño chili, seeded and finely chopped
2 Vidalia onions (about 1 pound), coarsely chopped
6-8 cloves garlic, minced
4 stalks celery, diced
3 pounds Roma tomatoes, diced
1 sprig fresh rosemary, chopped
3 leaves fresh basil, chopped
2 sprigs fresh thyme, chopped
Sea salt
Freshly ground black pepper

For the stuffing
1 tablespoon extra virgin olive oil
1 pound ground lamb
Sea salt
Freshly ground black pepper
2 large stuffing zucchini (about 1 1/2 pounds)
1 cup whole wheat bread crumbs
1 cup grated Parmesan cheese
Fresh flat-leaf parsley for garnish

To make the marinara, heat oil over medium heat in a large saucepan. Add jalapeño, onions, garlic, and celery. Cook until onions are translucent, about 5 minutes. Add tomatoes, rosemary, basil, thyme, salt, and pepper; cover. Simmer over low heat for approximately 2 hours, stirring occasionally.

Meanwhile, heat oil in a medium skillet over medium-high heat. Add ground lamb and stir so clumps do not form. Cook until no longer pink. Add meat to marinara sauce and blend well. Season with salt and pepper to taste.

Preheat oven to 400°. Line a baking sheet with unbleached parchment paper.

Cut zucchini in half lengthwise. Remove seeds and hollow out, leaving a 3-inch shell. Place zucchini halves on prepared baking sheet. Spoon meat and marinara sauce into zucchini halves. Bake for approximately 45 minutes, or until tender.

In a small bowl, mix together bread crumbs and cheese. Top each zucchini half with cheese mixture. Place under broiler; cook for approximately 3 minutes, until brown on top. Remove from oven and place on serving platter. Garnish with parsley.

My youngest sister, Maris Pascal, is an accomplished cook and has a kitchen to be envied by even the most accomplished chefs. Her kitchen island is larger than most people's kitchens, and all of her equipment is state of the art. While visiting her Greenwich home, Maris invited some of her friends over to dine with us and served this classic lamb dish. This is one of my all-time favorites and one typically found in Mediterranean homes. It is relatively easy to make, but a very elegant dinner for someone you love or for a dinner party.

Maris says the marinade should be the consistency of mayonnaise. I suggest serving this with glazed carrots, oven-roasted potato skins, and garden peas with fresh mint. Enjoy this healthy and delectable dinner!

Maris Pascal's Rack of Lamb
Serves 4

4 tablespoons Dijon mustard
1 cup extra virgin olive oil
3 tablespoons finely chopped fresh rosemary
2 large cloves garlic, minced
1 medium shallot, finely minced
1/8 cup white wine
Pinch of sea salt
1/4 teaspoon freshly ground black pepper
1 (8-bone) rack of *lamb* (about 1 1/2 pounds)

Place Dijon mustard in a medium-size bowl. Slowly whisk in olive oil (drizzle a little at a time) to emulsify. Add rosemary, garlic, shallot, white wine, salt, and pepper; whisk together. Place rack of lamb in a flat dish and fully coat both sides with marinade; cover; refrigerate for approximately 3 hours or more.

Preheat oven to 450°. Place lamb and marinade in a roasting pan. Cook for approximately 18-20 minutes, or until desired doneness; let sit for 5 minutes. Slice into individual ribs and serve.

Sisters (left to right): Maris, Jennifer and myself

Ever So Slightly Sweets

Friends and family have had to help me out on this chapter, as one is either a cook or a baker, and rarely both. I can bake, but it is not my favorite pastime. I confess that I love savory over sweet.

In the United States and Canada, cakes and pies are the traditional desserts served in our homes and restaurants. There is nothing like a piece of authentic apple pie with vanilla ice cream to comfort one's sweet tooth. In the Mediterranean countries (in fact, in most of the countries I have visited around the world), people often eat fresh fruit after dinner, which is probably one reason why they are trim. In Turkey, one might have whipped yogurt with honey and chopped nuts. The English love their trifles. India and the Middle East are famous for their rice puddings seasoned with ground cardamom. France has its famous Tarte Tatin, or upside down apple pie. In Spain, you will find different versions of crème caramel or Crème Catalan.

Children love to be in the kitchen when desserts are being prepared, perhaps one of the few times you'll find them willing to help out. Keep in mind that they will be perfecting their mathematical and scientific skills by measuring ingredients and learning how ingredients work together. And what child does not like to lick the pudding bowl!

Cayce was not one to *suggest* eating desserts, but he also encouraged us not to become too regimented in our diet. I guess *almost* everything in moderation is healthy, so enjoy an occasional dessert for a change of pace and a little fun. Cooked apples; fresh fruit pies, especially open-faced fruit pies; custards and puddings; and gelatin with fruits were mentioned in the readings as preferable to some other desserts.

Cayce also suggested walking a mile after dinner, and I think this is a great idea for a family, friends, or couples to do together, especially after eating dessert! Giving your body time to digest your meal before going to bed allows for a much better sleep, as well.

French Tarte Tatin
Cherry Clafouti
Marcus's Crème Brulee
Nanny's Snow Pudding and Custard Sauce
Whipped Yogurt and Cream with Honey
Suzie's One Bowl Cake
Cardamom Rice Pudding
Lola's Lemon Tart
Peaches and Honey Corn Bread
Cinnamon Applesauce
Zucchini Cake with Cream Cheese Icing
Strawberries and Jello
Coconut Ice Cream
Summer Fresh Fruit Tart
Cradle of Gold Carrot Cake

The famous and beautiful Loire Valley in France was once the seat of French nobility. At one point, there were more than 300 chateaux decorating this lush terrain of land. One summer, on a leisurely drive to a friend's home in Bretagne (Brittany), we toured this breathtaking area, staying in a charming bed and breakfast in Chenonceau. If you ever get a chance, read the fascinating history of this chateau. The 16th century in France was quite melodramatic and could rival our modern-day soap operas. This is where I first tasted this upside-down caramel tart and developed a love for its rich flavor.

The Tarte Tatin actually originated in this region. It was invented by one of the Tatin sisters totally by mistake in 1898 in their hotel restaurant. One day, lore has it, the eldest sister, Stephanie, inadvertently put the butter, apples, and sugar for her tart in a cast-iron skillet, over heat, without the pastry dough. Realizing that she had forgotten to line the skillet with the dough, she then added it on top and baked it in the oven.

I used to make my pastry dough from scratch and shuddered at the thought of buying a frozen one. However, now one can buy whole wheat dough, and it is actually quite remarkable. Suit yourself.

I think you will love this typical French dessert, and it will wow your family and guests.

You will need a well-seasoned, 10-inch, cast-iron skillet

French Tarte Tatin
Serves 6

1 frozen whole wheat puff pastry sheet, thawed
4 tablespoons (2 ounces) unsalted *butter,* softened
1/2 cup organic brown sugar
8 Golden Delicious *apples* (3-4 pounds), peeled, cored, and quartered

Preheat oven to 425°. Sprinkle work surface and rolling pin with flour. Roll pastry sheet into a 1/4-inch round. Place a dinner plate over pastry, and with a sharp knife, cut it into a 10- to 12-inch round. Place on a baking sheet and refrigerate until ready to use.

Place butter on the bottom and the sides of the skillet. Pour sugar evenly over the bottom, and arrange apples in a circular fashion on top of sugar; apples may come above the rim of the skillet. Cook apples in the skillet over medium-high heat, without stirring, for approximately 20-25 minutes, or until juices are a caramel color. Transfer skillet to a baking sheet, and bake in the oven for 20 minutes. Remove skillet from oven and place pastry dough over apples. Bake an additional 20 minutes, or until pastry is browned.

Place skillet on a baking rack, and allow to cool for 10-30 minutes. Prior to serving, invert a large, round platter and place on top of skillet. Invert the tart onto the platter and serve immediately.

Paula Reds apples from my sister and brother-in-law's orchards

Ever So Slightly Sweets

While living in Chamonix, France, I was introduced to this country-style pudding dessert by a neighbor and friend. I was quite surprised at the ease with which she made this and how delicious it was. French women know how to cook and have to be practical, as most of them also work. But they still believe in eating healthy meals and sitting down at the table to eat as a family.

This dessert can be served warm or room temperature and will keep for several days in the refrigerator. Cherries, plums, blueberries, pears, or peaches can be used or a mixture of whatever you fancy! My favorite is cherry clafouti, but depending on the time of year, use what is local and in season in your area. Of course, frozen fruit can be substituted if need be. Most recipes call for more sugar, but I don't think it's really needed. In fact, I love this version because it is not sugary sweet!

Cherry Clafouti
Serves 6

4 eggs
1 cup light cream
1 cup milk
1/2 cup organic unbleached white flour or gluten-free flour
1/4 cup organic beet sugar
1 teaspoon ground cinnamon
1/4 teaspoon pure vanilla extract
3 cups cherries, pits removed
Butter for greasing

Preheat oven to 375°. Generously butter a 12-inch gratin dish or other shallow ovenproof dish. In a large mixing bowl, beat the eggs, cream, milk, and vanilla. Whisk in the flour, sugar, and cinnamon until well blended. Line prepared baking dish with cherries; top with batter. Bake approximately 45 minutes, or until golden brown and set. Remove from oven and let cool for 10 minutes before serving.

Cherry Clafouti

Recently, good friends from Windsor, England, came for dinner. Both Shirley and Austen are former filmmakers, and I never tire of hearing their incredible stories about their travels and the movie stars they have worked with. Austin was a set designer and Shirley worked for the BBC for years. Their son is an acclaimed pastry chef. So instead of trying to impress any of them, I asked Marcus to supply the "pud" (pudding), as they say in England. I like to claim that I don't have a sweet tooth, but this is one of my favorite desserts.

Marcus's Crème Brulee
Serves 6

8 organic egg yolks
1/4 cup (2 ounces) organic caster sugar plus extra for topping
1 pint heavy cream
1 whole vanilla bean, split lengthwise and scraped, or 1 teaspoon pure vanilla extract

In a medium mixing bowl, whisk egg yolks and sugar until light in color; set aside. In a small, heavy saucepan, heat the cream and vanilla over medium-high heat until bubbles form at the edges. Take off heat and reduce heat setting to low. Immediately pour cream over yolk mixture, whisking as you pour. Transfer mixture to original saucepan, and stir continuously over heat with a spatula or wooden spoon until mixture has thickened slightly, enough to coat the back of the spoon or spatula. Be careful, otherwise the mixture will curdle! Pour back into mixing bowl, whisking, as this will take a little heat out of the mix and prevent curdling. Pour into 6 ramekins and refrigerate until set.

When the pudding is set and ready to serve, sprinkle with additional caster sugar and brown under the broiler or, better still, brown and crisp with a blowtorch. Voila!

Both my mum and my grandmother made this soothing dish for anyone who was feeling poorly. It is a beaten egg-white mixture, which resembles snow when put on a plate, covered with a custard sauce. It is a very light dessert and very soothing. This is also a great dessert for young children.

The custard sauce can be served warm or chilled, but it's especially lovely chilled. Add some fresh blueberries for extra nutrients and taste.

**Nanny's Snow Pudding and Custard Sauce
Serves 4**

For the snow
2 tablespoons Knox unflavored gelatin
1/4 cup cold water
1 cup boiling water
1 cup organic beet sugar
1/2 cup lemon juice
3 egg whites, stiffly beaten

Soak the gelatin in 1/4 cup cold water for several minutes. Add boiling water and stir to dissolve gelatin. Stir in sugar and lemon juice until the mixture thickens. Let rest while beating egg whites until stiff. Add gelatin mixture to egg whites, and beat again to ensure that gelatin mixture will not settle on the bottom. Refrigerate for several hours.

For the custard sauce
1 cup heavy cream
2 teaspoons vanilla extract
4 egg yolks
1/3 cup organic beet sugar

Begin to heat the cream and vanilla in a small, heavy saucepan over medium-high heat. While cream is heating, whisk together egg yolks and sugar in a small bowl until smooth. When the cream begins to bubble, temporarily remove the pan from heat. Slowly pour 1/2 cup of hot cream mixture into egg yolk mixture, whisking constantly. Gradually add egg yolk mixture to remaining cream mixture, whisking constantly. Return pan to heat and continue to cook over low- to medium-high heat, stirring constantly, until the mixture coats the back of a spoon.

To serve individually, place one-quarter of snow pudding on each dessert plate and top with one-quarter cup custard sauce. If using blueberries to accompany, place two tablespoons on each plate. For a more formal presentation, place snow pudding on a medium-size dessert platter with a border of fresh blueberries (if using). Serve custard sauce in a gravy bowl, and allow guests to pour it onto their own plates.

One of my most memorable vacations ever was with my family on a chartered sailboat, crossing the Aegean Sea from Rhodes, Greece, to the turquoise coast of Turkey. Our delightful crew consisted of a young South African couple and their best friend.

For two weeks, there were no telephones, faxes, or anything that could remind us of the outside world. At that time, Turkey was not a top tourist destination, so we got to see it before it became developed with large hotels. Bodrum, Fetiye, and Marmaris were some of our stops as well as other little-known ports.

Every day, our crew would ask us where we wanted to spend the night and what we wanted for dinner. It was magical. We had a windsurfing board, so we could take off at a moment's notice and sail freely, or just dive off the boat and swim. The crew prepared our meals for us with fresh food and ingredients purchased from local markets and dockside fishermen. One of the dishes I most loved was Turkish yogurt served with fresh honey. I can think of no better dessert to serve after a meal. Actually, this is a great way to start your day, as well.

Whipped Yogurt and Cream with Honey
Serves 4

2 cups low-fat or nonfat plain yogurt or soy yogurt
1/4 cup heavy cream or soy milk
1/4 teaspoon pure vanilla extract
4 tablespoons local honey

Place a mesh strainer or colander in a large bowl. Line with several layers of cheesecloth. Pour the yogurt over cheesecloth, cover, and refrigerate overnight. Discard the liquid in the bowl.

In a medium mixing bowl, whip the heavy cream with an electric mixer until soft peaks form. Continue whipping as you add the vanilla extract. Gently fold in the reserved yogurt. Pour equal amounts of yogurt and cream mixture into 4 dessert bowls or pretty glasses. Drizzle honey on top.

Variation: Replace honey with fresh fruit. Add toasted walnuts for crunch.

Ever So Slightly Sweets

My good friend Suzie Theo has a similar background to mine. (Her mum, Marianna, is my friend as well, and she has always been an inspiration to me.) Suzie's dad, a Romanian, worked in the hotelier business. For a time, the Theo family lived in Israel. They also made frequent trips to Europe to visit family in Romania, England, and Greece. I am happy that Suzie supplied this easy-to-make and gluten-free recipe, which is great served with fresh berries in the summertime.

Suzie's One Bowl Cake

1 1/4 cups oat flour
1 cup soy, rice, or spelt flour
4 teaspoons baking powder
1 teaspoon salt
3/4 cup organic beet sugar
1/2 cup sunflower oil
3/4 cup *soy* or *rice milk*
3 *eggs*
1 teaspoon vanilla (or other flavoring)
Whipped *cream* (optional)
Fresh fruit (optional)

Preheat oven to 350°. Line a 9-inch baking pan with unbleached parchment paper.

In a large mixing bowl, sift flours, baking powder, salt, and sugar. Add oil and milk; stir to blend. Add eggs and vanilla; blend all ingredients together. Pour batter into prepared pan. Bake approximately 25 to 30 minutes, or until a toothpick inserted into center of cake comes out clean. Let stand 5 minutes before turning out onto a cooling rack. Serve with homemade whipped cream, if desired, and your choice of fresh strawberries, blueberries, or sliced peaches.

I have come to love this dessert. Living in the Middle East made me realize how wonderful rice pudding can taste with the addition of ground cardamom—it lends an exotic touch. This silky dessert is very soothing when you're feeling under the weather. For those of you who like crunch, chopped pistachios make a yummy addition. Fresh fruit is equally delightful, when in season.

This pudding is often served in India (which I have yet to visit in this lifetime) and the Middle East.

Cardamom Rice Pudding
Serves 4

1/4 cup organic short-grain brown rice
2/3 cup *milk* or soy milk
3/4 cup *cream*
1 1/2 tablespoons beet sugar
1/4 cup golden raisins
1/4 teaspoon ground cardamom
Fresh berries (optional)

Preheat the oven to 150°. Lightly oil a one-quart ovenproof dish. In a medium bowl, mix the rice, milk, cream, sugar, raisins, and cardamom. Pour into prepared baking dish.

Bake the rice pudding for approximately 3 hours, or until the liquid has been absorbed and the pudding is creamy in texture. Serve with fresh berries, if desired.

Ever So Slightly Sweets

This is a classic lemon tart often featured in French restaurants or pastry shops, and my daughter Brooke's favorite. Her husband Yann thinks it is the best one he has ever tasted! People in America eat a similar one, only in smaller pie shells, or often enjoy a lemon meringue pie. I happen to prefer Lola's version, which is easily assembled and can be made a day ahead of any event you wish to serve it for. The luscious taste of lemon can be savored following dinner or with a cup of tea on a lazy afternoon.

Lola's Lemon Tart
Serves 8

9-inch pie crust
Lemon zest
5 lemons
5 *eggs*
1/4 teaspoon salt
1 cup beet sugar
3/4 cup *cream*
1/2 cup *butter,* melted

Preheat oven to 400°. Roll pastry on a lightly floured surface to fit a 9-inch pie plate. Place pastry in pie plate and prick with a fork. Cover pastry with dried beans; bake for 10 minutes. Remove beans; return pastry to oven for 10 minutes. Remove pastry from oven and allow to cool.

Meanwhile, zest 3 of the 5 lemons; set aside zest. Squeeze juice from the 5 lemons. In a small saucepan, bring juice to boil over high heat.

In a separate bowl, blend eggs, salt, sugar, and lemon zest with an electric mixer. Slowly pour in hot lemon juice, constantly mixing, until ingredients are incorporated. Pour ingredients into a small saucepan; cook over medium heat. Stir constantly until mixture thickens (enough to coat the back of a wooden spoon). Remove from heat. Pour in melted butter; blend well. Pour mixture into tart shell; cool. Cover and refrigerate for at least 3 hours or overnight.

Living in the South, I have learned to love corn bread. It is a staple in the diet here, and everyone seems to have a family recipe. However, I always like to create something new out of something old, so I made up this little dessert recipe days ago. The reaction from friends has been rather outstanding. Peaches are in season now, and on the way home from the Outer Banks, we stopped at one of our favorite farm stands, Tar Heel's Produce, to buy fresh peaches. They smelled so sweet and fragrant we bought lots of them. (Avoid buying peaches that have no scent—they should actually smell sweet—and they should be soft to the touch yet free of bruises.)

Whenever we come across a great farm market, we always stop to get the freshest produce and eggs possible. We stock up on whatever we find, not necessarily sure of what we intend to make, but we want only the best food and to help local farmers continue their noble work.

This corn bread is more a pudding than a corn bread and is oozing with honey sweetness. Traditionally, in the South, people cook their corn bread in a cast-iron skillet. I use a rectangular baking pan lined with unbleached parchment paper simply to make it easy to lift it out once cooked. This is also a more low-fat cooking method, as you do not need to grease the pan.

Peaches and Honey Corn Bread
Serves 8

1 ripe *peach,* peeled, pit removed, and sliced
1 tablespoon fresh lemon juice
1 cup organic cornmeal
1/3 cup unbleached white flour
1/4 teaspoon baking powder
1/4 teaspoon baking soda
1 *egg,* slightly beaten
1 cup *buttermilk*
4 ripe *peaches,* peeled, pit removed, and diced
1-2 tablespoons local honey for topping
Fresh mint leaves for garnish (optional)

Preheat oven to 350°. Line a 9-inch baking pan with unbleached parchment paper. Add lemon juice to sliced peach, and set aside until ready to serve corn bread.

Whisk together dry ingredients in a large mixing bowl. Mix in the egg and buttermilk. Pour half the batter into prepared baking pan. Top the batter with an even row of diced peaches. Add the rest of the batter. Bake for approximately 25 minutes, or until golden brown.

Remove from oven and score the top with a knife. Drizzle honey over corn bread. Allow to cool and cut into squares. Serve with reserved, fresh peach slices and fresh mint leaves.

Ever So Slightly Sweets

There is nothing better than homemade applesauce made with handpicked apples from a local farm. (PickYourOwn.org is a great Web site for finding farms nearby.) And, once again, supporting local farms is the way to go. It's also another fun way to spend an autumn day, bundled up, with family and friends in tow.

Making quantities of applesauce for canning is a superb idea—you can have it on hand year-round. Homemade applesauce is easy to make and a much healthier choice than a store-bought brand. If you choose the right varieties, no sugar is needed. Roma, Fuji, Gravenstein, and Golden or Red Delicious are great. I suggest a mixture of several varieties. Some people like their applesauce pureed until it is like velvet, but if you like a bit of chunk to it, do not overprocess. A hand-held immersion blender, a potato masher, or a food processor will help you attain your desired consistency. It is up to you whether you wish to peel the apples or not; I rather like the added fiber.

Cinnamon Applesauce

3 to 4 pounds *apples,* cored and quartered
1 strip lemon peel
Juice of 1 lemon
4-inch cinnamon stick
1 tablespoon honey

Put all ingredients in a large, heavy pot; cover and bring to a boil. Simmer 20 to 30 minutes, or until apples are soft. Remove lemon peel and cinnamon stick. Mash with potato masher, immersion blender, or food processor, depending on texture desired. Serve hot or cold.

Apples from my sister and brother-in-law's orchards

This cake is another great use for the abundance of zucchini in the autumn months. It is so mouthwatering you will want to have zucchini available all year long. This is one of those cakes that you can give to kids without their saying, "But I don't like zucchini!"—they'll never know such a delicious cake could be made from a vegetable. The cream cheese icing makes it even more melt-in-your-mouth delicious, but it's delicious with or without it.

Zucchini Cake with Cream Cheese Icing
Serves 8

1 cup beet sugar
2 eggs, slightly beaten
2 teaspoons vanilla
3 cups zucchini, grated
1 cup sunflower oil or vegetable oil
3 cups whole wheat flour or gluten-free flour
2 teaspoons baking soda
Pinch of salt
2 teaspoons ground cinnamon
1/4 teaspoon allspice
1 cup dried cranberries (optional)
1/2 cup chopped toasted walnuts (optional)

Cream Cheese Icing
2 cups low-fat cream cheese, room temperature
2 tablespoons pure maple syrup
Edible flowers for garnish (optional)

Preheat oven to 350°. Line 3 (9-inch) cake pans with unbleached parchment paper.

In a large mixing bowl, beat the sugar, eggs, and vanilla until light. Add the grated zucchini and oil; mix well. In a separate bowl, sift together the flour, baking soda, salt, cinnamon, and allspice. Add the dry ingredients to the zucchini mixture just until blended. Stir in cranberries and walnuts, if using. Pour cake batter into prepared pan. Bake in oven for approximately 25 to 35 minutes, or until a toothpick inserted into the center of the cake comes out clean. Allow to cool on a metal rack.

Meanwhile, make the icing. Place cream cheese and maple syrup in the bowl of food processor; process on high speed until creamy.

Once cake has cooled, remove unbleached parchment paper and place cake on cake dish. Carefully ice cake with a spatula. Place several toothpicks around top edge of iced cake; cover well and refrigerate if not serving within the hour. Bring to room temperature before serving, and garnish with edible flowers, if desired.

Ever So Slightly Sweets

Strawberries run wild in Pungo, Virginia, which is next door to where I live. Every summer, we locals wait with anticipation for strawberry season to start so we can go pick our own at one of the many farms in the area. Each year, there is the Pungo Strawberry Festival, which is held on Memorial Day. Not hundreds, but thousands of people attend this wonderful event, featuring all sorts of fun activities for children and we older children.

So here is a recipe for strawberry lovers—is there anyone who doesn't love this marvelous creation? It is simple and sweet and all things nice, and who wouldn't eat one's meal to have a plate of this?

Try using an old-fashioned mold to make an impressive presentation to bring to your table. Once jello is on a serving plate, a fun idea is to surround the jello with fresh strawberries and a bit of whipped cream to make it even more spectacular. Either way, this dessert will please most people.

Strawberries and Jello
Serves 8

2 packages strawberry jello
2 cups boiling water
2 cups cold water
2 cups chopped *strawberries*

In a large bowl, pour boiling water over jello. Stir and allow to sit for two minutes. Pour remaining two cups of cold water over mixture and stir. Once gelatin has started to gel, mix in chopped strawberries. At this point, leave it in the bowl, or pour it into your favorite mold. Cover tightly with plastic wrap and refrigerate until set.

Variation: Substitute strawberries with fresh peaches, pears, plums, or other fresh berries and a complementary flavored jello.

Strawberry picking in Pungo

In Asian countries, coconut milk replaces milk to make this smooth ice cream. This recipe is for the true coconut lover, and the key is to use fresh coconut meat, if possible. Coconuts can be opened with a hammer (watch your fingers!) and the meat scraped out. The difference in taste between packaged coconut flakes and fresh is just that—fresh!—however, fresh-frozen coconut flakes are now available in some grocery stores. Coconut milk can be found in most grocery stores and in abundance at Asian markets.

The ice cream can be frozen and served in hollowed out coconut shells, which makes for an authentic display on the table.

Note: If using an ice cream maker, follow the manufacturer's directions.

Coconut Ice Cream
Serves 4

4 cups unsweetened coconut milk
1/2 cup beet sugar
1/8 teaspoon almond extract
1 1/4 cups grated fresh coconut or unsweetened coconut flakes
1/4 cup toasted coconut flakes*

In a freeze-proof container, combine coconut milk and sugar; stir to dissolve sugar. Blend in almond extract and fresh coconut. Chill mixture in freezer for 4 to 5 hours, or until hardened. When ready to serve, top with toasted coconut flakes.

*To toast fresh coconut, place flakes in a single layer on a baking sheet and bake in a preheated 350° oven for 10-12 minutes, until golden brown. Stir several times to prevent burning.

This one-crust rustic tart is often served in Switzerland and France. As I am a rather lazy baker, this tart style appeals to me. Actually, it is as pretty as it is tasty. The effect of freshly baked seasonal fruit oozing out of a golden brown crust makes for a delightful picnic addition. Or, for an elegant dinner party ending, serve with vanilla ice cream, crème fraiche, or lightly whipped cream.

Summer Fresh Fruit Tart
Serves: 6

Short Crust Pastry
1 cup organic unbleached white flour
1/2 teaspoon salt
1/2 cup chilled butter
3 tablespoons ice water

Filling
2-pound mixture blackberries, raspberries, and peeled, sliced peaches,
1 tablespoon lemon juice
1 tablespoon honey
1/2 teaspoon cinnamon

Preheat oven to 375°. To make the pastry dough, blend salt and flour. Cut butter into flour, using a pastry cutter or with the aid of two knives, until mixture resembles bread crumbs. Stir in water a tablespoon at a time. Use just enough water that dough almost clings together. Wrap in wax paper and chill until ready to use.

Toss prepared fruit with lemon juice, honey, and cinnamon; set aside. Sprinkle work surface and rolling pin with flour. Roll out pastry into a 12-inch round; transfer to an ungreased baking sheet. Heap fresh fruit onto the pastry round, leaving a 2-inch, fruit-free border. Fold edges of pastry over fruit. Bake for approximately 35-40 minutes, or until pastry is golden brown.

Variation: Organic apples and pears may be substituted for fresh berries in the autumn months.

One of the most outstanding desert trips I took while living in Jeddah, Saudi Arabia, was to Mahd Adh Dhahab, or "The Cradle of Gold," also known as the site of the legendary gold mines of King Solomon. Driving through the rock-strewn and rough desert for 250 miles (400 kms) was not easy, and the directions were quite hilarious; for example, "fork in road—bear left." But what an experience for my very fortunate friends and me! Not many foreigners are given permission to do these types of trips in Saudi.

Waking up at dawn in our outdoor cots to see herds of camels with their babies in the distance; finding a desert oasis with hundreds of camels drinking from them, with a lone Bedouin watching them from his truck; cooking dinner over our makeshift barbeques; and falling asleep under billions of twinkling stars—these were not experiences to be taken for granted. What's more, two days after our arrival, we were invited by a group of 15 Swedish miners to join them for an *indoor* dinner at their campsite! The dinner was not gourmet, but to our group, the camaraderie of sharing homemade vegetable soup, bread and butter, a fatoush salad, and refreshing water and tea seemed like we were in a 5-star restaurant! The men were thrilled to have our company, being so far away from civilization, and we were overjoyed at being at a long camp table conversing with them. Remember, our campsite was the great outdoors . . .

As you might imagine, going down into one of the richest gold mines on earth and walking the 2-km. (about 1 1/4 miles) mine shaft to actually see gold was exhilarating. I guess I could go on and on about these experiences, but you would probably like to know about the food. . . Of course, to prepare for an adventure of this sort, everyone had to do his or her share, and that meant bringing food that could withstand such an arduous trip. One of the dishes I prepared was this yummy carrot cake, which keeps well and is great to take on any camping trip or picnic, near or far.

You will need an 11 x 7 x 2-inch pan

Cradle of Gold Carrot Cake
Serves 12-14

4 eggs
1 1/4 cups sunflower oil
2 cups beet sugar
2 teaspoons vanilla extract
2 cups organic unbleached white flour
2 teaspoons baking powder
2 teaspoons baking soda
1/2 teaspoon salt
1 teaspoon ground cinnamon
1 teaspoon ground ginger
1 teaspoon ground nutmeg
3 1/2 cups grated carrots
1 cup dried cranberries
1 cup golden raisins
1 cup pumpkin seeds (optional)

Preheat oven to 350°. Line an 11 x 7 x 2-inch rectangular baking pan with unbleached parchment paper.

In a large bowl, beat together eggs, oil, sugar, and vanilla. Using a sifter, sift in the flour, baking powder, baking soda, salt, cinnamon, ginger, and nutmeg. Stir in carrots, cranberries, raisins, and pumpkin seeds, if using. Pour into prepared baking pan.

Bake in oven for approximately 40 to 50 minutes, or until a toothpick inserted into the center of the cake comes out clean. Let cool in pan and then remove cake onto a wire rack; remove parchment paper. Cut into small squares and store in a cake tin.

Optional: Ice the cake with cream cheese icing (page 172) as you would the zucchini cake (page 172). Be sure to refrigerate if not serving within the hour.

Menu Suggestions

Hors d'Oeuvres
Tasty Tuna Pate
Smoked Salmon Canapés
Asian Pear, Gorgonzola, and Candied Walnut Canapés
New Potato Skins with Sour Cream and Rosemary
Crudités (Raw Vegetable Platter)
Green and Cured Olives
Whole Wheat Crackers

Wine and Cheese Party
Gruyere
Brie
Camembert
Maytag Blue Cheese
Saint Andre
Herb Encrusted Goat Cheese
Sharp White Cheddar Cheese
Dates, Toasted Walnuts, and Black Grapes
Whole Wheat Crackers
Pinot Noir, Chardonnay, and Pinot Grigio

Middle Eastern Picnic (Mezze)
Tabouleh
Fatoush
Black Bean Humus
Stuffed Peppers with Wild Rice
Feta Cheese with Olive Oil and Za'atar
Za'atar Pita Chips
Green and Cured Olives
Fresh Fruit
Mint Iced Tea

Summer Tea Party for Two or Twenty
Tomato, Mozzarella, and Basil Salad
Tea Sandwiches
Chicken Salad with Cranberries and Toasted Walnuts
Lou Lou's Lunar Tunar Salad
Cucumber with Fresh Mint and Butter
Cherry Clafouti
Iced Peach Tea with Fresh Basil

Summer Salad Buffet
Raw Beet and Orange Salad
Bree's Virginia Beach Summer Salad
Herbed Quinoa Salad
Summer Herb and Mixed Green Salad
Very Berry Gelatin Salad
Whole Wheat or Brown Bread
Lemonade and Iced Tea

Barbeque Party
Feta and Watermelon Salad
Sweet Potato Salad
Lamb Burgers
(Sliced Tomatoes and Onions)
Green Salad with Honey Mustard Vinaigrette
Fresh Fruit

Children's Birthday Party
Lopez Island Fish Tacos
Crudités (Raw Vegetables) with Ranch Dressing
Very Berry Lime Gelatin with Fresh Berries
Cradle of Gold Carrot Cake

Asian Buffet
Asian Slaw
Shrimp Pad Thai
Indonesian Chicken Satay with Peanut Sauce
Steamed Brown Rice
Honey and Ginger Glazed Carrots
Exotic Fresh Fruit Salad
Coconut Ice Cream

Elegant Dinner Party
Chilled Cucumber and Yogurt Soup
Grilled Salmon with Blueberry Coulis
Wild Rice
Honey and Ginger Glazed Carrots
Butter Beans with Fresh Mint
Steamed Yellow Squash with Herbes de Provence
Marcus's Crème Brulee

Italian Night Dinner
Bruschetta
Italian Rosemary Chicken
Zucchini Risotto
Glazed Carrots
Caesar Salad
Fresh Fruit

French Night Dinner
Field Greens with Toasted Chevre Salad
Coq au Vin
Brown Rice
Garden Peas
Tarte Tatin

Mediterranean Buffet Party
Mediterranean Fish Kabobs
Lebanese Chicken Za'atar
Fatoush
Rhodes Island Greek Salad
Mashed Sweet Potatoes with Za'atar
Fresh Fruit

1001 Nights Moroccan Dinner
Moroccan Carrot Salad
Chicken Tagine
Vegetarian Couscous
Garden Peas
Steamed Carrots with Cilantro Sprigs
Cardamom Rice Pudding

Vegetarian Dinner
Vegetarian Chili
Whole Wheat Irish Soda Bread
Rhodes Island Greek Salad
Fresh Fruit Tart

Vegan Dinner
Herb and Mixed Lettuce Salad with Citrus Vinaigrette
Roasted Beets with Beet Greens
Vegetarian Hotpot
Coconut Ice Cream
Fresh Fruit

Our Planet and Food

We have reached a time on our planet when we can no longer take things for granted—not the health of our food, our bodies, our planet, or our economy. I truly believe that the Edgar Cayce readings are filled with infinite wisdom—physical, mental, and spiritual—for these uncertain times. One of the practical suggestions Cayce made was to have a vegetable garden to help sustain us in case of financial hardship. And just by eating locally grown produce, as he suggested, you will be one step ahead in reducing your carbon footprint and in nourishing your body.

We have been feeling the effects of higher gas prices, higher grocery bills, and the stresses of a troubled economy. We have also been affected by the many recalls and cases of e-coli resulting from contaminated or overprocessed foods. People are starting to wake up to the importance of being aware of where their food comes from and supporting their local farmers, not only for health reasons (as the Cayce readings emphasize) or financial benefits but for ecological purposes—this is crucial.

Every early morning and afternoon talk show features food, and cooking has become a popular hobby. Chefs are now considered to be rock stars, and people of all ages, male and female, watch their shows on many networks. But much of the interest in diet has stemmed from a marked decline in our health and that of our children. In the Western nations, we are some of the wealthiest people on the planet, but sadly, also some of the most obese. The high rate of cancer, diabetes, and cardiovascular disease is making people take note of the importance of diet in disease prevention.

Eating organic, locally grown, and seasonal food is by far the most important gift you can give to your family, friends, loved ones, and yourself. Organic farms raise livestock humanely and with respect. They are allowed time out of doors, and they are not cramped together in their sleeping quarters.

Conventionally raised animals have a very sad life, on the other hand. They are taken from their mothers at a very young age, never see daylight, and often live in cramped spaces. They are injected with or fed hormones to make them grow faster and bigger. When taken to the slaughterhouses, they often have to travel in extreme heat or cold over very long distances. It makes me shudder to even think about it. Consumers are becoming more aware of cruelty to animals, and for this reason even some large food chains routinely provide free-range and organic meats, poultry, and eggs.

At the Friday Souk, near Marrakech, I actually saw the outside of a slaughterhouse where Berbers had come down from the mountains on foot, by donkey or, if they were lucky, in a truck to sell their wares and animals to be killed for food. What amazed me was the respect the animals were given before being killed. The people actually bless them, as it is done in the Orthodox Jewish religion. Native Americans also practice this habit, and I am sure other cultures do, as well. I know the meat from these animals tastes better and is better for us because of this.

Just as we wish to be treated with respect and dignity, so do the animals that supply us with this source of protein.

There is much debate today on the subject of GMOs (genetically modified organisms) in our food chain. Chemical pesticides are spliced into cells of plants to increase crop yields. Corn and corn products, wheat, rice, and soy and soy products are predominantly GMO-produced in the United States farming system. We have no idea of the health risks involved by consuming these new breeds of foods. One example is that industrial tomato plants are crossed with fish genes so that they will be resistant to colder weather. By eating organically grown products, however, you can be sure that you will not be consuming an abundance of pesticides or other organisms. There are many Web sites that explain in depth the negative aspects of GMO foods.

Surely, we can no longer afford to saturate our soils with artificial fertilizers that force plants to grow quickly. In industrialized nations, between 300 and 500 agrochemical pesticides are stored in the average adult body at one time. Added to that, chemical food additives are used by manufacturers to improve store shelf life. And, as we know, the antibiotics and hormones that are routinely fed to or injected into livestock are in turn passed on to their human consumers. According to the British Medical Association, "The risk to human health of antibiotic resistance is one of the major health threats that could be faced in the 21st century."

Another vital global concern is the state of our oceans and waterways. Fertilizers used in farming flow into rivers and end up in our oceans, polluting them and infecting the sea life in them. And the human population's appetite for fish is driving many species to the point of extinction.

How to reduce our individual and national carbon footprint is a huge point of discussion today. An excellent first step is to use public transportation instead of personal vehicles to get around. Or walk or ride a bicycle—which is also a wonderful way to exercise and to enjoy being out of doors. There are convenient Web sites under *RideShare.com*, if you are interested, that will help you connect with local people who wish to carpool. More and more people are opting for this relaxing way to get to work and to avoid the hassle with traffic. There are also community Web sites for families that would like to carpool their children. The amount of mileage, mechanical expense, and gasoline saved by making some of these changes is fast becoming a new trend for people who are ecologically minded, and a necessary measure for those who have been forced to reduce spending.

There is also a great Web site called *LocalHarvest.com*, which will provide lists of farms, CSAs (Community Supported Agriculture), and co-operatives in your local area. By typing in the name of your city or your area code, all farms within that region will magically appear, including directions on how to get there. Instead of eating foods that have lost their taste after being shipped thousands of miles, drive to your local farm to choose freshly picked vegetables and fruits and free-range eggs, poultry, and meats. You are not only supporting small businesses but saving your family a lot of expense.

By joining a CSA, you are supporting a local farm. Literally, you become a shareholder, and in exchange for your financial commitment, you receive a basket of in-season fruits and vegetables from that farm weekly. It is tremendously rewarding to receive your bounty. Some CSAs require members to work a certain number of hours on the farm, which is great physical activity. And what a wonderful opportunity to teach children where their food is coming from and not to take it for granted. Also, they will be more inclined to try new vegetables if they get their hands dirty planting them!

Finally, I cannot emphasize enough how important it is to sit down together as a family at mealtime. Studies have shown that children are much more inclined to discuss issues and topics that they would not discuss otherwise if left on their own to eat their meals. We can all benefit from this extra time to connect with one another. And take time to chew your food slowly. This is good for your digestion and helps you to know when you have eaten enough. If you gobble your food down, your stomach does not have time to tell you it is full. Savor every bite.

The best advice I can give anyone is to make food with *love* and take the time to go back to the old ways of doing things—but with a new twist! By sitting down with your family to a home-cooked meal, you are sharing something that money cannot buy. And, it is hoped, you are helping to avoid medical issues later in life. You are helping to save our planet by saving yourselves!

Index

A

Anchovy:
    Mediterranean Anchovy Vinaigrette, 70

Anchovy Paste:
    Juliette Caesar's Salad Dressing, 64

Appetizers:
    Black Bean Humus, 5
    Bruschetta, 11
    Canapés, 13
        Asian Pear Canape, 16
        Cheddar Cheese and Marmalade, 18
        Feta Cheese Canape, 14
        Grilled Portobello Mushroom Canape, 15
        Smoked Salmon Canape, 13
    Chunky Guacamole, 10
    Feta Cheese Dip, 6
    Herbed Soft Cheese Dip, 8
    Jennifer's Christmas Eve Cheese Mountain, 12
    Mango and Black Bean Salsa, 21
    New Potato Skins with Sour Cream, 17
    Raita, 7
    Tahini Lemon Dipping Sauce, 19
    Tasty Tuna Pate, 4
    Vegetarian Pizza, 20
    Za'atar Pita Wedges, 9

Apple(s):
    Cinnamon Applesauce, 171
    French Tarte Tatin, 162

Apricot(s):
    Algerian Apricot Lamb, 156
    Moroccan Chicken Tagine, 141

Asian Pear:
    Asian Pear Canape, 16
    Exotic Fresh Fruit Salad, 54

Avocado:
    Caesar Salad, 40
    Chunky Guacamole, 10
    Tomato and Mozzarella Stack, 33

B

Bacon:
    South African Spinach Quiche, 102

Bean(s):
    Black Bean Humus, 5
    Black Bean Soup, 81
    Indian Spiced Kale and Garbanzo Beans, 106
    Mango and Black Bean Salsa, 21
    Vegetarian Chili, 93

Bean Sprouts:
    Chop Suey, 110
    Shrimp Pad Thai, 131

Beet(s):
    Raw Beet and Orange Salad, 48
    Roasted Beets and Sauteed Beet Greens, 115
    Shaved Fennel and Beet Salad, 49

Berries: *Also see specific berries*
    Mixed, 47
    Very Berry Lime Gelatin, 47

Blackberry(ies):
    Summer Fresh Fruit Tart, 175

Black currants:
    Turkish Cabbage Dolma, 103

Blueberry(ies):
    Blueberry Coulis, 122

Bread:
    Bruschetta, 11
    Crostini, 11
    Peaches and Honey Corn Bread, 170

Broccoli:
    Broccoli and Sunflower Seed Salad, 30
    Chop Suey, 110
    Vegetable Stir Fry, 109

Butter:
    Parsley Butter, 124

Butter Beans:
    Very Vegetable Soup, 85

Buttermilk:
    Beautiful Blue Cheese Dressing, 72
    Chilled Cucumber and Dill Soup, 87
    Ranch Dressing, 73

C

Cabbage:
    Asian Slaw, 51
    Chop Suey, 110
    Turkish Cabbage Dolma, 103

Cake:
    Cradle of Gold Carrot Cake, 176
    Suzie's One Bowl Cake, 167

Canape:
    Asian Pear, 16
    Cheddar Cheese and Marmalade, 18
    Feta Cheese, 14
    Grilled Portobello, 15
    Smoked Salmon, 13

Carrot(s):
    Asian Slaw, 51
    Black Bean Soup, 81
    Chop Suey, 110
    Cradle of Gold Carrot Cake, 176
    Curried Couscous and Chicken Salad, 52
    Grilled Vegetables, 113
    Honey and Ginger Glazed Carrots, 107
    Moroccan Carrot Salad, 41
    Moroccan Carrot Soup, 88
    New Year's Day Fish Chowder, 84
    Tunisian Vegetarian Couscous, 100
    Vegetable Stir Fry, 109
    Vegetarian Chili, 93
    Very Berry Lime Gelatin, 47

Cauliflower:
    Chop Suey, 110
    Vegetable Stir Fry, 109

Celery:
    Black Bean Soup, 81
    New Year's Day Fish Chowder, 84
    Shitake and Wild Mushroom Soup, 82
    Vegetarian Chili, 93
    Very Berry Lime Gelatin, 47
    Very Vegetable Soup, 85
    Virginia Crab Bisque, 83

Cheese:
    Asian Pear and Blue Cheese Canape, 16
    Beautiful Blue Cheese Dressing, 72
    Brooke's Grilled Eggplant, 105
    Cheddar Cheese and Marmalade Canape, 18
    Feta and Watermelon Salad, 35
    Feta Cheese Canape, 14
    Feta Cheese Dip, 6
    Herbed Soft Cheese, 8
    Jennifer's Christmas Eve Cheese Mountain, 12
    Toasted Goat Cheese Salad, 34
    Tomato and Mozzarella Stack, 33

Cherry:
    Cherry Clafouti, 163

Chicken:
    Argentinian Chimichurri Chicken, 151
    Celestial Chicken Salad, 43
    Chicken with Forty Cloves of Garlic, 139
    Chicken with French Cream Sauce, 145
    Cilantro Chicken, 147
    Coq au Vin, 146
    Curried Chicken, 149
    Curried Couscous and Chicken Salad, 52
    Indonesian Chicken Satay, 150
    Italian Rosemary Chicken, 138
    Japanese Chicken Yakatori, 148
    Lebanese Chicken Za'atar, 144
    Mexican Chicken Fajitas, 140
    Moroccan Chicken Tagine, 141
    Sesame Chicken with Peach Salsa, 142
    Sweet Potato Chip Encrusted Chicken, 143

Chili:
    Vegetarian Chili, 93

Coconut:
    Coconut Ice Cream, 174

Coconut Milk:
    Curried Chicken, 149
    Outer Banks Fish Chowder, 90
    Thai Shrimp Soup, 89

Court Bouillon:
    Lake Geneva Perch Filets, 126

Couscous:
    Curried Chicken and Couscous Salad, 52
    Moroccan Chicken Tagine, 141
    Tunisian Vegetarian Couscous, 100

Crab:
    New Year's Day Fish Chowder, 84
    Seafood Quesadillas, 130
    Virginia Crab Bisque, 83

Cranberries:
    Celestial Chicken Salad, 43
    Southern Sweet Potato Salad, 31
    Wild Rice Salad, 32

Cream:
    Cherry Clafouti, 163
    French Cream Sauce, 145
    Marcus's Crème Brulee, 164
    Mushroom Sauce, 132
    Nanny's Snow Pudding and Custard Sauce, 165
    South African Spinach Quiche, 102
    Suzie's One Bowl Cake, 167
    Whipped Yogurt with Cream and Honey, 166

Cream Cheese:
    Creamy Zucchini Soup, 86
    Herbed Soft Cheese Dip, 8
    Tasty Tuna Pate, 4
    Zucchini Cake with Cream Cheese Icing, 172

Cucumber(s):
    Chilled Cucumber and Dill Soup, 87
    Fatima's Fatoush Salad, 38
    Middle Eastern Taboule, 37
    Rhodes Island Greek Salad, 39
    Salade Nicoise, 42
    Wilderness Mango Salad, 36

Curry:
    Curried Chicken, 149
    Curried Couscous and Chicken Salad, 52

D

Daikon:
    Asian Slaw, 51

Date(s):
    Moroccan Chicken Tagine, 141
    Tunisian Vegetarian Couscous, 100

Desserts:
    Cardamom Rice Pudding, 168
    Cherry Clafouti, 163
    Cinnamon Applesauce, 171
    Coconut Ice Cream, 174
    Cradle of Gold Carrot Cake, 176
    French Tarte Tatin, 162
    Lola's Lemon Tart, 169
    Marcus's Crème Brulee, 164
    Nanny's Snow Pudding and Custard Sauce, 165
    Peaches and Honey Corn Bread, 170
    Strawberries and Jello, 173
    Summer Fresh Fruit Tart, 175
    Suzie's One Bowl Cake, 167
    Whipped Yogurt and Cream with Honey, 166
    Zucchini Cake with Cream Cheese Frosting, 172

Dips:
    Feta Cheese, 6
    Guacamole, 10
    Herbed Soft Cheese, 8
    Raita, 7

Dressings and Vinaigrettes:
    Dressings:
        Ah-So Asian, 68
        Beautiful Blue Cheese, 72
        Fifi's French, 66
        Juliette Caesar's, 64
        Lola's Lemon Tahini, 67
        Mayonnaise, 74
        Ranch, 73
        Zola"s Greek, 71
    Vinaigrettes:
        Anais's Red Wine, 60

Balsamic, 58
Bree's Citrus, 59
Mediterranean Anchovy, 70
Really Roasted Red Pepper, 62
Roberta's Raspberry, 61
Totally Tomato, 63
Wonderful Watercress, 69
Yodeling Yogurt, 65

Dried Cranberry:
Celestial Chicken Salad, 43
Southern Sweet Potato Salad, 31
Wild Rice Salad, 32

Duck:
Roast Duck with Orange Sauce, 153

E

Edible Flowers, xix

Eggplant:
Autumn Ratatouille, 98
Brooke's Grilled Eggplant, 105

F

Feta:
Bree's Virginia Beach Salad, 50
Feta and Watermelon Salad, 35
Feta Cheese Canape, 14
Feta Cheese Dip, 6
Rhodes Island Greek Salad, 39

Fennel:
Shaved Fennel and Beet Salad, 49

Fish:
Anchovy Vinaigrette, 70
Asian Salmon Cakes, 133
Asian Shrimp Skewers with Peanut Sauce, 127
Baked Halibut with Parsley Butter, 124
Canadian Seafood Newburg, 120
Flounder with Pesto, 129
Grilled Salmon with Blueberry Coulis, 122
Grilled Tuna with Lemon Marinade, 125
Lake Geneva Perch Filets, 126
Lopez Island Fish Tacos, 121
Mediterranean Fish Kabobs, 128
New Year's Day Fish Chowder, 84
Outer Banks Fish Chowder, 90
Poached Salmon with Remoulade, 123
Seafood Quesadillas, 130
Shrimp Pad Thai, 131
Steamed Mussels in Wine, 134
White Fish with Mushroom Sauce, 132

Flounder:
Flounder with Pesto Sauce, 129

Fowl:
Asian Turkey Burgers, 152
Roast Duck with Orange Sauce, 153

Fruit: *See also specific fruits*
Exotic Fresh Fruit Salad, 54
Summer Fresh Fruit Tart, 175
Summer Fruit Quinoa Salad, 29
Winter Fruits and Nuts Quinoa Salad, 29

G

Garbanzo Beans:
Indian Spiced Kale and, 106

Gelatin:
Lime Gelatin with Grated Vegetables, 46
Nanny's Snow Pudding and Custard Sauce, 165
Strawberries and Jello, 173
Very Berry Lime Gelatin, 47

Green Bean:
Tunisian Vegetarian Couscous, 100
Vegetarian Chili, 93

H

Halibut:
Baked Halibut with Parsley Butter, 124
Lopez Island Fish Tacos, 121

Herbs,
Herbes de Provence, recipe, xx

Honey:
Honey and Ginger Glazed Carrots, 107
Peaches and Honey Corn Bread, 170
Whipped Yogurt with Honey and Nuts, 166

I

Ice Cream:
    Coconut, 174

J

Jello:
    Lime Gelatin with Grated Vegetables, 46
    Strawberries and Jello, 173
    Very Berry Lime Gelatin, 46

K

Kale:
    Indian Spiced Kale and Garbanzo Beans, 106

Ketchup:
    Fifi's French Dressing, 66

Kiwi fruit:
    Exotic Fresh Fruit Salad, 54

L

Lamb:
    Algerian Apricot Lamb, 156
    Jane's Jazzy Lamb-Stuffed Zucchini, 157
    Lancashire Lamb Hot Pot, 155
    Maris Pascal's Rack of Lamb, 158
    Middle Eastern Lamb Burgers, 154

Leek:
    Vegetable Stock, 78
    Very Vegetable Soup, 85

Lemon:
    Citrus Vinaigrette, 59
    Grilled Tuna with Lemon Marinade, 125
    Lebanese Mashed Potatoes, 116
    Lola's Lemon Tart, 169

Lentils:
    Lentil Shepherd's Pie, 112

Lime:
    Lime Gelatin with Grated Vegetables, 46
    Very Berry Lime Gelatin Salad, 46

Lobster:
    New Year's Day Fish Chowder, 84

M

Mango:
    Mango and Black Bean Salsa, 21
    Wilderness Mango Salad, 36

Maple Syrup:
    Asian Pear Canape, 16
    Zucchini Cake with Cream Cheese Icing, 172

Mayonnaise:
    Beautiful Blue Cheese Dressing, 72
    Fifi's French Dressing, 66
    homemade, 74
    Remoulade, 123

Melon:
    Chilled Melon Soup, 91
    Feta and Watermelon Salad, 35

Menus, 177

Mussels:
    Steamed Mussels in Wine, 134

Mushroom(s):
    Coq au Vin, 146
    Grilled Vegetables, 113
    Portobello Mushroom Canape, 15
    Shitake and Wild Mushroom Soup, 82
    Vegetable Stir Fry, 109
    Vegetarian Pizza, 20
    White Fish with Mushroom Sauce, 132
    Wild Mushroom Ragout, 108

N

Nuts::
    Celestial Chicken Salad, 43
    Jennifer's Christmas Eve Cheese Mountain, 12
    Raw Beet and Orange Salad, 48
    Sesame Noodle Salad, 45
    Shrimp Pad Thai, 131
    Southern Sweet Potato Salad, 131
    Toasting Nuts and Seeds, 24
    Turkish Cabbage Dolma, 103
    Winter Fruits and Nuts Quinoa Salad, 29

O

Olive:
    Feta and Watermelon Salad, 35
    Feta Cheese Canape, 14
    Rhodes Island Greek Salad, 39
    Salade Nicoise, 42

Orange:
    Raw Beet and Orange Salad, 48
    Winter Fruits and Nuts Quinoa Salad 29

P

Paella:
    Vegetarian, 99

Parsnip:
    Vegetable Stock, 78

Pastry Dough:
    Summer Fresh Fruit Tart, 175

Pea(s):
    Curried Couscous and Chicken Salad, 52
    Vegetarian Paella, 99

Peach:
    Peaches and Honey Corn Bread, 170
    Peach Salsa, 142
    Summer Fresh Fruit Tart, 175
    Summer Fruit Quinoa Salad, 29

Peanut: *See Sauces, Peanut*

Peanuts:
    Shrimp Pad Thai, 89

Pepper(s):
    Andalusia Gazpacho, 92
    Asian Slaw, 51
    Autumn Ratatouille, 98
    Mediterranean Fish Kabobs, 128
    Mexican Chicken Fajitas, 140
    Really Roasted Red Pepper Vinaigrette, 62
    Stuffed Peppers with Wild Rice, 111
    Vegetable Stir Fry, 109
    Vegetarian Hotpot, 101
    Vegetarian Paella, 99
    Vegetarian Pizza, 20

Perch:
    Lake Geneva Perch Filets, 126

Pie(s):
    French Tarte Tatin, 126
    Lentil Shepherd's Pie, 112
    Lola's Lemon Tart, 169
    Summer Fresh Fruit Tart, 175

Pineapple:
    Exotic Fresh Fruit Salad, 54

Pizza:
    Vegetarian, 20

Polenta:
    Grilled Portobello Mushroom Canapés, 15

Potato(es):
    Lebanese Mashed Potatoes, 116
    New Potato Skins with Sour Cream, 17

Poultry: *See Chicken and Fowl*

Q

Quiche:
    South African Spinach Quiche, 102

Quinoa:
    Herbed Quinoa Salad, 28
    Summer Fruit Quinoa Salad, 29
    Winter Fruits and Nuts Quinoa Salad, 29
    Very Berry Lime Gelatin, 47

R

Raisins:
    Broccoli and Sunflower Seed Salad, 30
    Cardamom Rice Pudding, 168
    Lou Lou's Lunar Tunar Salad, 44
    Stuffed Peppers with Wild Rice, 111
    Tunisian Vegetarian Couscous, 100
    Winter Fruits and Nuts Quinoa Salad, 29

Raspberry(ies):
- Roberta's Raspberry Vinaigrette, 61
- Summer Fresh Fruit Tart, 175
- Very Berry Lime Gelatin, 47

Rice:
- Cardamom Rice Pudding, 168
- Stuffed Peppers with Wild Rice, 111
- Turkish Cabbage Dolma, 103
- Vegetarian Paella, 99
- Wild Rice Salad, 32
- Zucchini Risotto, 104

Rice Noodles:
- Shrimp Pad Thai, 131

S

Salads:
- Asian Slaw, 51
- Bree's Virginia Beach Salad, 50
- Broccoli and Sunflower Seed Salad, 30
- Caesar Salad, 40
- Celestial Chicken Salad, 43
- Curried Couscous and Chicken Salad, 52
- Exotic Fresh Fruit Salad, 54
- Fatima's Fatoush Salad, 38
- Feta and Watermelon Salad, 35
- Herbed Quinoa Salad, 28
- Lime Gelatin with Grated Vegetables, 46
- Lou Lou's Lunar Tunar Salad, 44
- Middle Eastern Tabouleh, 37
- Moroccan Carrot Salad, 41
- Raw Beet and Orange Salad, 48
- Rhodes Island Greek Salad, 39
- Salade Nicoise, 42
- Sesame Noodle Salad, 45
- Shaved Fennel and Beet Salad, 49
- Sienna's Summer Salad, 53
- Southern Sweet Potato Salad, 31
- Summer Fruit Quinoa Salad, 29
- Toasted Goat Cheese Salad, 34
- Tomato and Mozzarella Stack, 33
- Very Berry Lime Gelatin Salad, 47
- Wilderness Mango Salad, 36
- Wild Rice Salad, 32
- Winter Fruits and Nuts Quinoa Salad, 29

Salsa:
- Mango and Black Bean Salsa, 21

Salmon:
- Asian Salmon Cakes, 133
- Grilled Salmon with Blueberry Coulis, 122
- Poached Salmon with Remoulade, 123
- Smoked Salmon Canapé, 13

Sauces:
- Blueberry Coulis, 122
- Chimichurri, 151
- French Cream Sauce, 145
- Mushroom Sauce, 132
- Orange, 153
- Peanut, 150
- Pesto, 129
- Yakatori, 148

Scallops:
- New Year's Day Fish Chowder, 84
- Seafood Quesadillas, 130

Seafood: *Also See Fish*
- Anchovy Vinaigrette, 70
- Asian Salmon Cakes, 133
- Asian Shrimp Skewers with Peanut Sauce, 127
- Baked Halibut with Parsley Butter, 124
- Canadian Seafood Newburg, 120
- Flounder with Pesto, 129
- Grilled Salmon with Blueberry Coulis, 122
- Grilled Tuna with Lemon Marinade, 125
- Lake Geneva Perch Filets, 126
- Lopez Island Fish Tacos, 121
- Mediterranean Fish Kabobs, 128
- New Year's Day Fish Chowder, 84
- Outer Banks Fish Chowder, 90
- Poached Salmon with Remoulade, 123
- Seafood Quesadillas, 130
- Shrimp Pad Thai, 131
- Steamed Mussels in Wine, 134
- White Fish with Mushroom Sauce, 132

Seeds:
- Bree's Virginia Beach Salad, 50
- Broccoli and Sunflower Seed Salad, 30

Lou Lou's Lunar Tunar Salad, 44
Sesame Chicken with Peach Salsa, 142

Shrimp:
    Asian Shrimp Skewers and Peanut Sauce, 127
    Canadian Seafood Newburg, 120
    Seafood Quesadillas, 130
    Shrimp Pad Thai, 131
    Thai Shrimp Soup, 89

Snow Peas:
    Asian Slaw, 51
    Vegetable Stir Fry, 109

Soba Noodles:
    Sesame Noodle Salad, 45

Soups:
    Andalusia Gazpacho, 92
    Black Bean, 81
    Chicken Stock, 79
    Chilled Cucumber and Dill, 87
    Chilled Melon Soup, 91
    Creamy Zucchini, 86
    Fish Stock, 80
    Moroccan Carrot, 88
    New Year's Day Fish Chowder, 84
    Outer Banks Fish Chowder, 90
    Shitake and Wild Mushroom, 82
    Thai Shrimp, 89
    Vegetable Stock, 78
    Vegetarian Chili (with the veggies!), 93
    Very Vegetable Soup, 85
    Virginia Crab Bisque, 83

Soy Nut:
    Asian Slaw, 51

Spinach:
    Grilled Portobello Mushroom Canapés, 15
    South African Spinach Quiche, 102

Squash:
    Grilled Vegetables, 113
    Very Vegetable Soup, 85

Strawberries:
    Strawberries and Jello, 173
    Very Berry Lime Gelatin, 47

Stocks:
    Chicken, 79
    Fish, 80
    Vegetable, 78

Sun-Dried Tomato(es):
    Really Roasted Red Pepper Vinaigrette, 62

Sweet Potato:
    Asian Salmon Cakes, 133
    Lancashire Lamb Hotpot, 155
    Lentil Shepherd's Pie, 112
    New Year's Day Fish Chowder, 84
    Oven-Roasted Sweet Potatoes, 114
    Salade Nicoise, 42
    Southern Sweet Potato Salad, 31
    Sweet Potato Chip Encrusted Chicken, 143
    Vegetarian Chili, 93
    Vegetarian Hotpot, 101

T

Tahini:
    Lola's Lemon Tahini Dressing, 67
    Tahini Dressing, 67
    Tahini Lemon Dipping Sauce, 67

Tofu:
    Shrimp Pad Thai, 131
    Thai Shrimp Soup, 89

Tomato(es):
    Andalusia Gazpacho, 92
    Autumn Ratatouille, 98
    Bruschetta, 11
    Fatima's Fatoush Salad, 38
    Outer Banks Fish Chowder, 90
    Shrimp Pad Thai, 131
    Tomato and Mozzarella Stack, 33
    Totally Tomato Vinaigrette, 63
    Vegetarian Chili, 93
    Vegetarian Pizza, 20

Tortillas:
    Mexican Chicken Fajitas, 140

Tuna:
    Bree's Virginia Beach Summer Salad, 50
    Canadian Seafood Newburg, 120
    Grilled Tuna with Lemon Marinade, 125
    Lou Lou's Lunar Tunar Salad, 44
    Mediterranean Fish Kabobs, 128
    Salade Nicoise, 42
    Tasty Tuna Pate, 4

Turkey:
    Asian Turkey Burgers, 152

V

Vegetable(s):
    Autumn Ratatouille, 98
    Brooke's Grilled Eggplant, 105
    Chop Suey, 110
    Grilled Vegetables, 113
    Honey and Ginger Glazed Carrots, 107
    Indian Spiced Kale and Garbanzo Beans, 106
    Lebanese Mashed Potatoes, 116
    Lentil Shepherd's Pie, 112
    Oven-Roasted Sweet Potatoes, 114
    Roasted Beets and Sautéed Beet Greens, 115
    South African Spinach Quiche, 102
    Stuffed Peppers with Wild Rice, 111
    Tunisian Vegetarian Couscous, 100
    Turkish Cabbage Dolma, 103
    Vegetable Stir Fry, 109
    Vegetarian Hotpot, 101
    Vegetarian Paella, 99
    Very Vegetable Soup, 85
    Wild Mushroom Ragout, 108
    Zucchini Risotto, 104

W

Watercress:
    Lime Gelatin with Grated Vegetables, 46
    Sienna's Summer Salad, 53
    Wonderful Watercress Dressing, 69

Water Chestnut:
    Chop Suey, 110

Watermelon:
    Feta and Watermelon Salad, 35

Y

Yam:
    Outer Banks Fish Chowder, 90

Yogurt:
    Herbed Soft Cheese Dip, 8
    Raita, 7
    Tahini Lemon Dipping Sauce, 67
    Whipped Yogurt and Cream with Honey, 166
    Yodeling Yogurt Dressing, 65

Z

Za'atar:
    Lebanese Chicken Za'atar, 144
    Lebanese Mashed Potatoes, 116
    Za'atar Pita Wedges, 9
    Za'atar, recipe, xx

Zucchini:
    Creamy Zucchini Soup, 86
    Curried Couscous and Chicken Salad, 52
    Grilled Vegetables, 113
    Jane's Jazzy Lamb-Stuffed Zucchini, 157
    Vegetable Stir Fry, 109
    Vegetarian Chili, 93
    Zucchini Cake with Cream Cheese Frosting, 172
    Zucchini Risotto, 104

A.R.E. Press

The A.R.E. Press publishes books, videos, audiotapes, CDs, and DVDs meant to improve the quality of our readers' lives–personally, professionally, and spiritually. We hope our products support your endeavors to realize your career potential, to enhance your relationships, to improve your health, and to encourage you to make the changes necessary to live a loving, joyful, and fulfilling life.

For more information or to receive a free catalog, call:

800-333-4499

Or write:

A.R.E. Press
215 67th Street
Virginia Beach, VA 23451-2061

ARE Press.com

Edgar Cayce's A.R.E.

What Is A.R.E.?

The Association for Research and Enlightenment, Inc., (A.R.E.®) was founded in 1931 to research and make available information on psychic development, dreams, holistic health, meditation, and life after death. As an open-membership research organization, the A.R.E. continues to study and publish such information, to initiate research, and to promote conferences, distance learning, and regional events. Edgar Cayce, the most documented psychic of our time, was the moving force in the establishment of A.R.E.

Who Was Edgar Cayce?

Edgar Cayce (1877-1945) was born on a farm near Hopkinsville, Ky. He was an average individual in most respects. Yet, throughout his life, he manifested one of the most remarkable psychic talents of all time. As a young man, he found that he was able to enter into a self-induced trance state, which enabled him to place his mind in contact with an unlimited source of information. While asleep, he could answer questions or give accurate discourses on any topic. These discourses, more than 14,000 in number, were transcribed as he spoke and are called "readings."

Given the name and location of an individual anywhere in the world, he could correctly describe a person's condition and outline a regimen of treatment. The consistent accuracy of his diagnoses and the effectiveness of the treatments he prescribed made him a medical phenomenon, and he came to be called the "father of holistic medicine."

Eventually, the scope of Cayce's readings expanded to include such subjects as world religions, philosophy, psychology, parapsychology, dreams, history, the missing years of Jesus, ancient civilizations, soul growth, psychic development, prophecy, and reincarnation.

A.R.E. Membership

People from all walks of life have discovered meaningful and life-transforming insights through membership in A.R.E. To learn more about Edgar Cayce's A.R.E. and how membership in the A.R.E. can enhance your life, visit our Web site at EdgarCayce.org, or call us toll-free at 800-333-4499.

Edgar Cayce's A.R.E.
215 67th Street
Virginia Beach, VA 23451-2061

EDGARCAYCE.ORG